How to Create Wealth on a Salary

How to Create Wealth on a Salary

Getting Your Withholding Back and Other Legal Tricks

DICK LEVIN
Associate Dean
Graduate School of Business Administration
University of North Carolina

GINGER TRAVIS
Contributing Editor

LAMBERT DER
Cartoonist

Prentice Hall, Englewood Cliffs, New Jersey 07632

Library of Congress Cataloging-in-Publication Data

Levin, Richard I. (date)
How to create wealth on a salary : getting your withholding back and other legal tricks / Dick Levin ; contributing editor, Ginger Travis ; cartoonist, Lambert Der.
p. cm.
Includes index.
ISBN 0-13-404534-3
1. Investments—Law and legislation—United States—Popular works. 2. Investments—United States. 3. Finance, Personal—United States. I. Travis, Ginger. II. Title.
KF1070.Z9L478 1988
346.73'092—dc 19 87-33410
[347.30692] CIP

Editorial/production supervision
and interior design: Sophie Papanikolaou
Cover design: Lundgren Graphics, Ltd.
Manufacturing buyer: Lorraine Fumoso

©1988 by Prentice-Hall, Inc.
A Division of Simon & Schuster
Englewood Cliffs, New Jersey 07632

All rights reserved. No part of this book may be reproduced, in any form or by any means, without permission in writing from the publisher.

The publisher offers discounts on this book when ordered in bulk quantities. For more information, write:

Special Sales/College Marketing
Prentice-Hall, Inc.
College Technical and Reference Division
Englewood Cliffs, NJ 07632

Printed in the United States of America

10 9 8 7 6 5 4 3 2 1

ISBN 0-13-404534-3

Prentice-Hall International (UK) Limited, *London*
Prentice-Hall of Australia Pty. Limited, *Sydney*
Prentice-Hall Canada Inc., *Toronto*
Prentice-Hall Hispanoamericana, S.A., *Mexico*
Prentice-Hall of India Private Limited, *New Delhi*
Prentice-Hall of Japan, Inc., *Tokyo*
Simon & Schuster Asia Pte. Ltd., *Singapore*
Editora Prentice-Hall do Brasil, Ltda., *Rio de Janeiro*

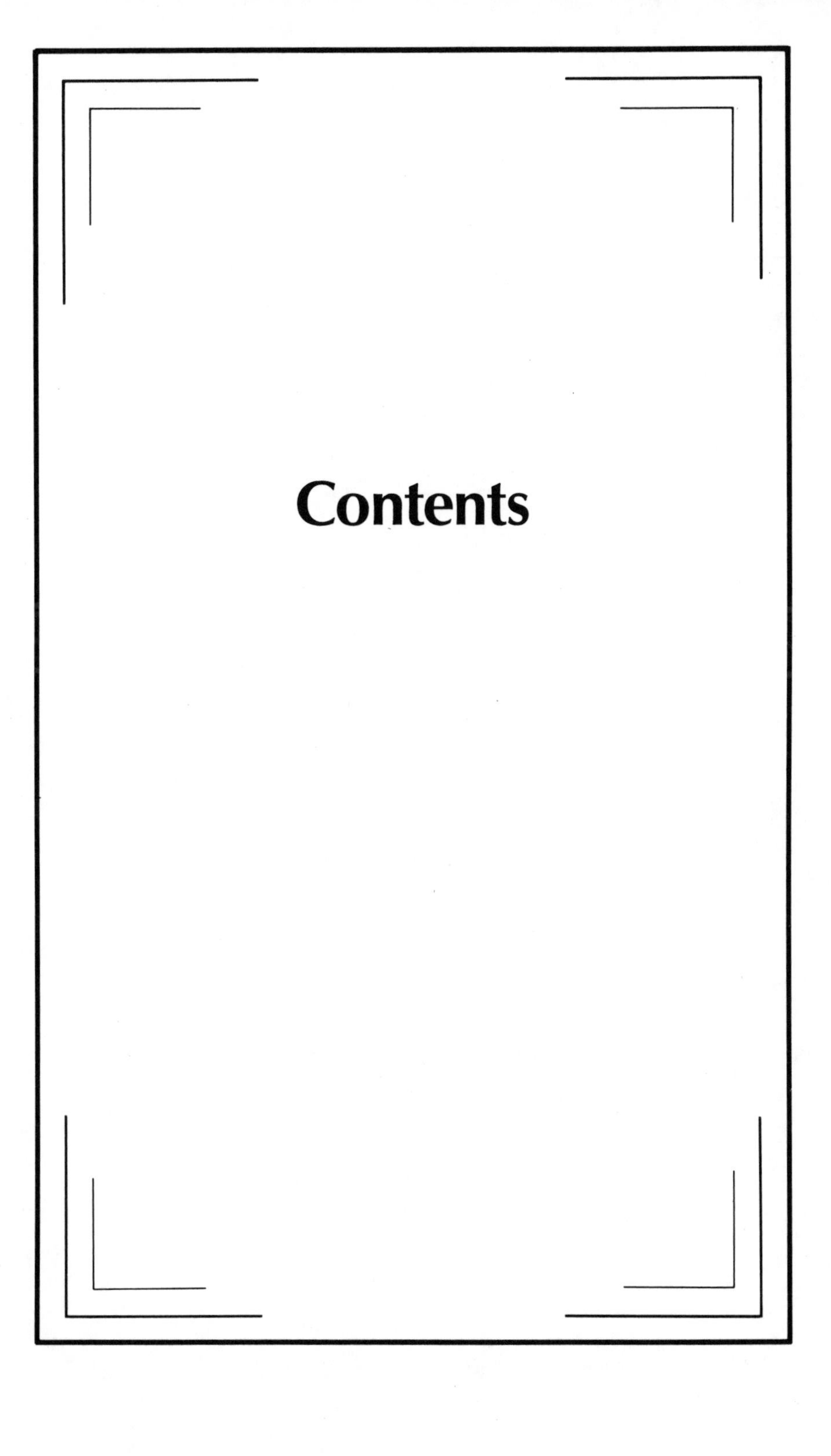

Contents

IV DEALS FOR SALARIED FOLK TO BE WARY OF

V WEALTH CREATION AS A FAMILY AFFAIR

VI WRAP, CAVEATS, DREAMS

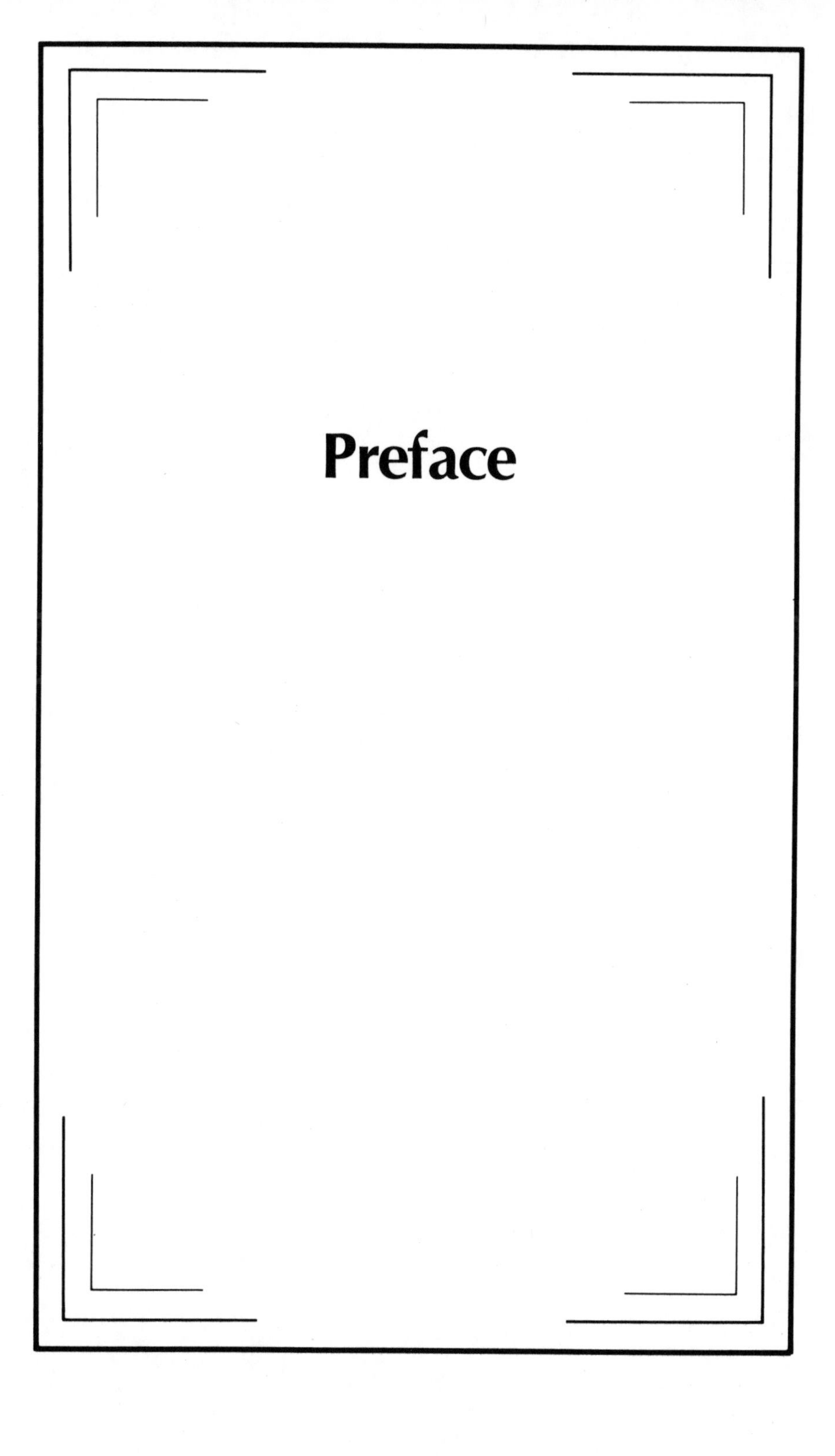

Preface

Hello. This book is really about two topics. The last eight chapters are about what (and what *not*) to invest in to create wealth on a salary. The first seven chapters are about everything else (what it takes to create wealth, what wealth really is, how much to invest, how to increase what you can invest, how to do the fancy numbers the financial types can do, what you need to know about income taxes, why your banker is not always your friend, whether and when you need experts to help you, and why I married Charlotte).

The first seven chapters are *very* important. If you are serious about creating wealth on your salary, you should read these seven chapters carefully (maybe even twice) before you take even one teeny, weeny look at the last eight chapters. If you are the kind of person who turns to the back of mystery novels, you will probably read the last eight chapters first. You will then be unhappy, confused, lost (most of the time), mad at yourself, mad at me, and you will probably tell all of your friends, which means I will sell fewer books.

On the other hand, if you are the type of person who *first* reads and rereads the list of characters in the front of *War and Peace,* or who conscientiously checks the parts list *before* starting to assemble something from a kit, then you and I will get along famously. I think you'll learn something useful here. You'll have a good time doing it, and, all other things being equal, you will wind up with more money than the "other kind."

Before we start, we need to be honest with each other. Practically everyone knows that the only ways to accumulate great wealth these days are to marry it, rob a bank, start a new religion, or sell drugs. However, when you look carefully at the divorce rate, the high numbers of bank failures, the departure of the Baghwan Rashneesh, and the condition of Latin American jails, maybe you should read the book anyhow.

Everything else that was on my mind follows.

Dick Levin

How to Create Wealth on a Salary

1

Getting Started

I have been poor and I have been rich. Rich is better. SOPHIE TUCKER

HUMILITY 1940s STYLE

When I was a kid in this little one-horse Southern town in the 1940s, I remember a black man who died and left over $100,000 (about a million dollars, inflation-adjusted, in today's money) mostly to his church. Mind you, none of this was insurance . . . it was all in the bank. At the time, I was working in the local drugstore making 15¢ an hour and my father was a traveling salesman making about $100 a week. I was pretty good at arithmetic, so the comparisons were easy and the lesson profound.

Now, blacks in the South back then didn't own many businesses; this man (whose name was Sim) worked for wages in a local plant, couldn't read but could sign his name, never earned more than $50 a week in his entire life, and accumulated this wealth at a time when interest rates were less than half of what they are today. He never owned stock, he rented the house he died in, and he had one suit and seven kids. One of his kids, Charles, dug fishing worms for a nickel a can, and Sim's wife "took in washing" (as they used to call it) and managed the family garden.

Sim would have liked this book. He wouldn't have been able to read it (the forties were long before *Brown* v. *the Board of Education*), but he would have understood it because he lived it, and that's more important. Sim had brains, guts, discipline, and a few dreams. If you pass Sim's test, stay with us—we may have something for you.

WHO THIS BOOK IS FOR (PARDON THE SYNTAX)—DICK'S SCHTICK

This book is aimed squarely at the segment of the population (the gang, in other words) who are salaried and earn an annual individual or family income between $20,000 and $70,000. Now that range is anything but a random choice. I believe that if you earn less than $20,000 a year today, the cost of life's necessities makes it difficult for you just to get by. In that case, if you have a couple of extra bucks, I feel you just ought to blow it—that's right, buy a few beers, get that new dress or leather jacket, take off for Myrtle Beach for the weekend, trade in the old car—anything but worry about creating wealth. In high-class financial terms, at twenty grand, you're not getting much joy, and sacrificing any of the little bit you *are* getting for the value of some undetermined amount of wealth ten or twenty years hence just doesn't make good sense. (However, if you're determined to accumulate monetary wealth—as opposed to the kinds money can't buy—you might look for a job that will let you do it.)

On the other hand, if you and your spouse or significant other are taking in *more* than, say, $70,000 a year, you can afford to play investment games that are just not going to be part of *this* book. At that level of income, you may find my financial homilies too conservative and too tame . . . and I would understand if you did! For example, $85,000 is enough to live on nicely, "play" the market, and still be able to take a shot at the financial brass ring once in a while—including maybe even an occasional wild pass at commodity futures, rare stamps, and penny stocks.

At $35,000 a year, however, the stock market is just not for you. There are other strategies I'll show you that will get you where you want to be, and with a lot fewer ulcers too! So there's the schtick, market-segmented all nice and neat, tied up and packaged: salaried men and women earning annual family incomes between $20,000 and $70,000 who score three out of four on brains, guts, discipline, and a few dreams. I'm sorry not to accommodate you high rollers, real estate tycoons, art collectors, wild-assed entrepreneurs, and gold arbitragers, but then there are 250 other books for you, some cheaper than this one. One of

my college friends, who says he's made and lost more money in the market than most folks, kids me about writing a book like this. If I ever write a book about his kind of investor, it'll be called *How to Make a Million Dollars in the Stock Market: Start with Two Million.*

WHO THIS BOOK IS FOR: OTHER IMPORTANT CRITERIA

So you earn $53,750—is this book for you? Only if you pass three more tests, so step right up for Dr. Dick's examination. First, what are your risk-taking proclivities? (And I don't mean unsafe sex.) If you're still reading, you probably don't believe in the tooth fairy, and in your heart of hearts you don't buy any "get-rich-quick-on-a-dime" promises. But are you ready to buy my maxim that you can't create wealth without taking *some*, albeit very modest, risk? What kind of risk? you ask. Fair enough question. Would the thought of losing two months' rent on a duplex you bought next door scare the hell out of you? Step down if the answer is yes. Would you come apart if we had you invested in Ginny Maes (mortgage investments guaranteed by the U.S. government and about as safe as the American flag) and rising interest rates next year reduced the value of your portfolio by 5 percent? Go to the back of the line if you answered yes. If you can't stand *these* and similar levels of risk, what you need to do is leave your money in a savings account and let it accumulate at about 6 per cent a year, but be sure you pick a bank that will *never* fail. I'm not going to advise you to do anything that will get you in trouble financially, but neither will I ask you to believe that there is anything left in this world without some risk, including eating your mom's apple pie. (What if the orchard was planted over a hazardous waste dump? You've got to *think* about these things.)

Second, I'm going to assume that you are a *professional* and that your primary professional focus is keeping your position and advancing in your organization, and that you have already discovered that to accomplish that successfully you need to concentrate at least forty-five hours a week on your job. If you have a full-time job that you do in twenty hours a week, then the assumptions I make about you in this book are simply not real. The wealth-creation strategies to come all assume that you work for a living and don't have thirty hours a week left over to manage your investments. (Not true? Try *Turning Leisure Time into Millions.)*

And finally, the most important of these three criteria—your family! (Equally important are your extended family and friends if you're single.) I'll always assume that your family and friends come *ahead* of your wealth-creation strategy, and that you won't do something stupid like tell your spouse, kids, significant other, or friends that you can't spend much time with them for the next five years because you need to make a lot of money so you can enjoy being with them later. I'm not going to suggest anything in here that takes a lot of time away from the family or from the people who are important to you. This is not a book about how to live your life backwards. So if people come before money in your priorities, then you're reading the right book. Cleared all the hurdles and still with us? Hang on, here we go!

PREVIEW OF WHAT'S COMING

Here's a quick scan of the chapters to follow:

The second chapter in our two-chapter series on getting started is

- *Chapter 2: Wealth Creation as a Mindset* What wealth really means (different strokes for different folks); ways in which wealth is created; why discipline is such an important part of a wealth strategy; measuring risk and return before you invest; overcoming inertia and fear as an investor; and learning to do something new—what's the best way.

A five-chapter sequence follows, covering the fundamentals you need to know about creating wealth:

- *Chapter 3: How Much Are You In For and How to Boost the Ante* How much can you afford to play for psychologically; how much can you afford financially—figuring out all the demands on your income and ciphering up your "investable residual"; boosting your investable residual by cutting expenses; over a hundred simple ways to cut your cost of living but not the fun; and look how much you can invest now!
- *Chapter 4: Becoming a Quant Jock in Five Easy Steps* Compound interest, the best thing since Doonesbury; rates of wealth accumulation; setting wealth-creation goals and testing them to see if you are being realistic; getting comfortable figuring out where you are and where you will be.
- *Chapter 5: An Income-Tax Primer* What does income tax mean to you; a short history of income tax; tax savings, tax deductions—what is the difference; after-tax equivalents, what they mean for you; what the Feds will and won't let you do; the difference between being legal and being stupid (*very* important).

- *Chapter 6: Banks Can Be Bad for Your Wealth* Who bankers are; how they are trained; why you have to interact with them; how they get promoted; how to approach them; how to use competition in banking to get a better deal; working with more than one bank; don't sign away your firstborn; limiting personal liability; recourse and non-recourse loans; your banker is not necessarily your friend.
- *Chapter 7: You and the Experts* Why most of us need a CPA; the folly of doing our own taxes given the way Congress and the IRS behave; how to manage your CPA; why most walk-in tax services just won't do what you need; financial advisors, who they are; interviewing one, embarrassing questions to ask; how they make money; why you need to make this decision very very carefully.

Next, we have four chapters on wealth creation strategies made to order for folks like you.

- *Chapter 8: Deals That Are Really Hard to Beat (IRAs, Keoghs, Company-matching Deals)* IRAs and why they are still good for you; Keogh plans and why they make you wealthier; company-matched deals as the nearest thing to a free lunch you'll ever see; goodies for teachers and employees of tax-exempt organizations.
- *Chapter 9: Safe Stuff—The Kind You Never Have to Worry About* Bank account balances are safe but watch out; money market stuff and CDs; government securities, what they are; how many kinds there are; how to buy them; what you get; safety versus return.
- *Chapter 10: Investments You Don't Pay Any Tax On* What tax-frees are; why they are tax-free; risk-return revisited; figuring your taxable equivalent rate of return the easy way; who these are for.
- *Chapter 11: Real Estate—The Kind You Can Reach Out and Touch* What's unique about real estate investments; safe rather than sorry; leverage that works for you; what to buy; the house next door, the duplex down the block; doing the numbers; how to manage what you buy profitably; don't for-

get why you own it; get the family involved in management to save taxes.

Now on to two chapters describing wealth creation strategies that don't make as much sense for you but that you ought to understand.

- *Chapter 12 Owning a Piece of a Company, A Piece of a Company's Debt, or a Piece of a Piece of Something* What these investments really are; how much folks really make in the securities markets; what the risks are; why this is probably not your cup of tea; what to buy if you absolutely positively have to play; what to avoid; the man (woman) who never sold a stock; the woman (man) who never bought one; why these scare the hell out of me; the great October 1987 crash.
- *Chapter 13: Life Insurance, as an Investment, You Generally Have to Die to Win* What it is; how you really win; the investment return in life insurance; why you should buy only two kinds of insurance; whom to insure; why you should never insure kids; being pragmatic; but she sells it so well.

Next, we have a few interesting and useful ideas on how to get the whole family in on the wealth creation deal.

- *Chapter 14 Getting the Family in the Act* Why this is a great wealth creation strategy; how it's done; tax-deferred income; how to get your spouse self-employed; what differential tax rates mean for your wealth creation strategy; how kids can play; taking off big piles and putting on smaller piles; parents as gift givers; what to give as gifts and why; new tax laws.

Finally, we have a chapter that wraps everything up, ties it with a bow, and sends you off with a bag of dos and don'ts.

- *Chapter 15 Looking Back; Looking Around; Looking Ahead* What we have been saying for fourteen chapters; what kinds of deals make sense for you; what kinds of deals to avoid like the plague; how to get started; how to see thin spots in the ice; brains, guts, discipline, and a few dreams; peace.

THE TOOTH FAIRY I AM NOT

By now, you know why I didn't call this book *The 60-Second Investor* or *How I Made $1,000,000 in My Spare Time.* If it sounds too good to be true in your world and mine, it is. Yet there are tens of thousands of bright, honest, hard-working people today who still believe in the financial tooth fairy—people who believe stocks only go up, who believe they can create real wealth in real estate with nothing down, who run around looking for the million-dollar potential of these undiscovered antiques in this little old lady's attic, and who listen up real hard when someone pitches them on "this little business worth a fortune." That schtick always sells well; it's the Fantasy Island of wealth creation. Meanwhile, back here in Peoria . . .

Wealth creation for the salaried person with an annual income between $20,000 and $70,000 is *not* easy (inheriting money, starting a new religion, or robbing a bank are all easier), but it's do-able! How?

FIRST, REMEMBER SIM

Brains, guts, discipline, and a few dreams.

Second, no jerking the family around and don't do anything to jeopardize your job.

Third, say bye-bye to the tooth fairy. Let's get to work. Wealth, here we come!

2

Wealth Creation as a Mindset

There is no wealth but life. JOHN RUSKIN

The dollars aren't important—once you have them. JOHNNY MILLER

WHAT'S A MINDSET?

Mindset is a term I learned from Jim Key, a former MBA student (which goes to show how we professors really operate—we borrow folks' watches so we can tell other folks what time it is). "Mindset," Jim said, "is where your head is at, what you pay attention to, how you think."

Creating wealth on a salary takes a mindset—the set of values, the focus, and the thinking to make the decisions you have to make. Sim had the right mindset (raised to at least the third power), but most folks don't, for reasons both in and out of their control.

A FEW NUMBERS

In 1980, the U.S. Census Bureau did its first-ever study of wealth in the United States. The Census Bureau reported that the typical U.S. family had a net worth of $32,667. (Net worth means what you own—assets—less what you owe—liabilities. If you own more than you owe, bless you, your net worth is positive.) Note that the typical family's net worth in the 1980s is only a third of what Sim's was back in 1940.

MORE FIGURES

If you are white, your net worth rises to $39,135; if you are Hispanic, it falls to $4,913; and if you are black (like Sim), it drops all the way down to $3,397. These are what they call "median figures"—that is, half of the folks in the United States are above you and half below you. Households headed by a woman had a net worth of only $13,890.

And where were all these dollars stashed? The study says that of all accumulated wealth, 41 percent was accounted for by equity in a home. Another 17 percent of the median family's net worth was deposited in interest-bearing accounts in banks and other financial institutions, while only 7 percent was in stocks or mutual funds.

A few quick conclusions:

- A net worth of $32,667 for the median family is awful. Sim did three times that much without an education, the *Wall Street Journal,* or the tax-shelter benefits of owning his own home.
- Wealth is *very* irregularly distributed in the United States. If you are white, yours is likely to be over ten times as much as if you were black. And what you read about the disproportionate percentage of women and children in poverty is true. Lots of folks start from way behind where you are (assuming you had the discretionary income to buy this book), and they deserve credit for keeping their car running and their kids fed—and real admiration if they pull off Sim's feat: starting poor but ending wealthy.
- If you pass Sim's test (brains, guts, discipline, and a few dreams), it really doesn't make much difference whether you read the study or whether you're black, white, red, or polka-dot! You *can* create wealth at a rate much better than the "median family." And you still might even have time to do a little fishing to keep your head straight.

MINDSET: HAVE YOU GOT IT? CAN YOU GET IT?

You *can.* More than anything else, it's a matter of focus—deciding what you want and then going after it. Anybody can learn *how,* but not everybody wants to go after it.

For example, suppose I make this very modest proposal to your friend Roger: "Rog, I can help you put together a portfolio of wealth totaling a quarter of a million dollars on your current earnings if you'll show me that you can increase your monthly savings by $200." And Rog says, "Dick, hey, I'd love to, man, but I haven't got the change to spare. My car and boat payments alone, Dick, are like some people's mortgages. And I gotta have a *little* fun!" Okay, so call it either lack of interest or lack of discipline, but Roger just hasn't got the mindset right now. He's a lot of fun, though. And maybe he'll get it later.

So we'll try Sue. Sue's star is shining at work; she's a medical administrator, good at it, getting noticed. Works *hard*. "Sue, I can tell you how to accumulate $400,000 *before* you're too old to enjoy it. Among other things, you've got to stop putting all your money in a passbook savings account and buy that nice-looking duplex near your apartment." And Sue says, "Dick, I'm real busy right now and besides I've never owned any real estate, don't want to go in debt to my eyeballs, don't want the hassles, don't want the commitment and—real estate's pretty risky isn't it? But I might ask my father what he thinks. I'll let you know, okay?" So Sue's got some hurdles to cross before she gets the mindset: (1) overcoming her fear of the unknown, and (2) managing her own money without male approval. Give Sue five years—she's got possibilities.

And you? You could create a net worth of $750,000—it may be do-able at your age and earning power—but you'd have to try some new investments (not very risky ones, mind you), do a few other new things, save a bit money, adjust your lifestyle modestly to create additional investable funds, and read and sign some papers now and then. You will? You're ready? All right! You've got the mindset to take us both where we want to go!

WHAT'S WEALTH MEAN TO DIFFERENT FOLKS, ANYHOW? (OR, HOW MUCH IS ENOUGH?)

To our friend Sim of Chapter 1, wealth meant enough money to give his church more than anyone else had ever given. It was simple to figure out the amount and a snap for Sim to check how he was doing from time to time. (The hard part was *doing* it.)

To an old flying friend of mine named Pebbly, wealth meant having enough money to eat twice a day, keep an old car going, and pay for a couple of hours of flying every week. Don't laugh at Pebbly too quickly; when he died, it was with a smile and an incredible nonduplicatable set of memories about flying small planes at sunset and at dawn. Those were worth at least a million dollars in anybody's money. Pebbly's cash equivalent wealth was zero when he expired, but that's just not the kind of wealth some folks count.

I'm in the writing business, and so are a lot of my friends. I have one good friend in particular whose ideas about wealth are worth listening to. She wants to own a small house in the country, a truck that always runs, a stack of dry firewood to hold her through the coldest winter, a job that lets her practice her profession without "giving or taking any shit," enough cash to buy a new banjo, and to be on someone's Blue Cross plan. She's got most of it except the Blue Cross, and she's gaining on that.

At the other extreme in decimal places are people such as J. Paul Getty, Armand Hammer, and the Rockefellers, who have so much money that wealth for them no longer has anything to do with their standard of living or primary needs. They have no problems with housing, food, entertainment, or, for heaven's sake, getting on anyone's Blue Cross plan. If they want to see the sunset in a private plane, any one of the company's $12 million jets will do nicely. And they already have a nice little place in the country—actually in several countries. So wealth to these people means something entirely different from what it does to you or me. It doesn't make them any more willing to part with a nickel, but neither does it make them any less contributors to society.

And what of the 400,000 folks (I hope!) who buy this book and who earn between $20,000 and $70,000? What does wealth mean to them and to you? Is it eating your way through France and staying at castles in Spain? Skiing in Aspen? Reef diving in Australia? Is it a college education for your kids at $50,000 a pop, or an elderly parent who needs $1,500 a month to live in a nursing home? Is it starting a business of your own, or the freedom, finally, to tell your boss "to take this job and shove it"? Is it your own secure retirement? Is it a week at the beach every year, a month at the beach, or your own cottage at the beach? Is it a trip to see your sister in California whom you haven't seen in three years, making it to your tenth college reunion, taking your significant other out for an elegant meal at the best restaurant in town, having your own home gym, buying a nice set of golf clubs for your brother, giving $1,000 to your church or synagogue, joining a club, buying wine by the case, having a regularly scheduled massage, getting your hair cut in New York, buying a sailboat, paying off your Visa card so they quit charging you interest, getting your teeth capped or your nose fixed, or a million other expressions of wealth?

Wealth is what wealth is to *you*, not to me or anyone else.

Don't ever forget that. Some folks get off financially by accumulating millions, while others believe that if you like what you do, get paid for it, have your health, love someone, and wind up the month with ten bucks, you *are* wealthy. Of course, you may be able to do all those nice things and wind up the month with a million bucks, too. Takes all kinds!

WHAT'S WEALTH FOR—SHORT LIST

Wealth is for spending or leaving. If you spend it, you can spend it meticuously, shepherding every penny, or you can just throw it away on whatever strikes your fancy. It's your money. If you leave it, you can leave it to your kids or your siblings, or—forget them!—leave it to the National Foundation for the Preservation of Turkey Callers. It's your money. Mostly, though, wealth is for causing security and/or happiness either now or in the future. The trick is not to wait to enjoy what you've got right now, even as you put money aside for later. (Or even if you decide *not* to put money aside for later.) Poverty is *no* fun and that includes poverty of spirit. Wealth, however *you* count it and enjoy it, sure feels better.

A further point: In your pursuit of wealth, don't deny yourself everything so you can use your wealth when you retire. If you do that, you will be old, grumpy, disappointed, and weird-looking as you suddenly try to recapture lost youth at age 75. Spend some money as you go through life, not as a wastrel, but sensibly. Buy yourself a new wardrobe, move to a new apartment, and save some bucks too. You're a smart person. Figure out what experiences make sense now and look foolish at age sixty, and then figure out what experiences will be great at sixty and inappropriate now. Then live the best life now that is appropriate for your age and bank account. When you're sixty, do the same thing again. You will spend much less on therapy this way!

Here's some anecdotal evidence that this method really works: Way back when I was twenty-four, a young married man with one kid and another coming, I was driving home from an out-of-town trip one day and saw this fantastic 1932 B-model

Ford roadster, chopped and channeled, full-modified block, white convertible top, which would do 90 mph in second gear. I borrowed $1200 and bought it on the spot. When I got home, I shared the same logic with my bride, Charlotte, that I just did with you . . . something about behavior being age-appropriate and all that. She was very pregnant, very uncomfortable, very short of money, and *very* unimpressed. Fortunately, after thirty-seven years of marriage, she has forgiven me and now I can ply this same logic on others.

HOW MUCH WEALTH PASSES YOUR WAY?

Most of us live long enough to earn some real money for about forty years. I mean something beyond delivering newspapers and working at Wendy's on weekends. If you stop to calculate how much you actually earn in this forty-year working phase, it's staggering. Look at Table 1, on page 20, which shows the money that comes your way (at least for a while on payday) over several different working periods.

When you look at it this way, the "median net worth" of $32,667 for the United States looks even worse. A bit of quick arithmetic puts that figure in perspective. For our $20,000-a-year earner, at, say, the end of twenty-five years of working (probably where the median U.S. wage earner is), a net worth of $32,667 is only

$$\frac{\$32{,}667 \text{ (their net worth)}}{\$500{,}000 \text{ (earnings after 25 years)}} \times 100\% = 6.5\%$$

which loosely interpreted means that after twenty-five years of work, this person is worth only 6.5 percent of everything he or she has earned. Where's the rest? Spent, dear reader! Meticulously and legally parceled out or just thrown away, but spent nonetheless!

But $20,000 is only the bottom range. Suppose you've been working for twenty years at very respectable average earnings of $3,500 a month, which is $42,000 a year, and suppose you've put

Table 1

If You Earn This Much a *Month*	This much money will come your way this many years					
	15 years	20 years	25 years	30 years	35 years	40 years
$1667 (our $20,000/year reader)	$300,000	400,000	500,000	600,000	700,000	800,000
$2000	$360,000	480,000	600,000	720,000	840,000	960,000
$2500	$450,000	600,000	750,000	900,000	1,050,000	1,200,000
$3000	$540,000	720,000	900,000	1,080,000	1,260,000	1,440,000
$3500	$630,000	840,000	1,050,000	1,260,000	1,470,000	1,680,000
$4000	$720,000	960,000	1,200,000	1,440,000	1,680,000	1,920,000
$4500	$810,000	1,080,000	1,350,000	1,620,000	1,890,000	2,160,000
$5000	$900,000	1,200,000	1,500,000	1,800,000	1,950,000	2,400,000
$5500	$990,000	1,320,000	1,650,000	1,980,000	2,310,000	2,640,000
$5833 (our $70,000/year reader)	$1,050,000	1,400,000	1,750,000	2,100,000	2,450,000	2,800,000

together a net worth (assets less liabilities) of, say, $110,000. Then your calculation goes like this:

$$\frac{\$110{,}000 \text{ (your net worth)}}{\$840{,}000 \text{ (your earnings after 20 years)}} \times 100\% = 13\%$$

Not as shabby as 6.5 percent, but not nearly what it could be.

One more time: Suppose you've done very well salarywise, as they say, and have averaged $5,000 a month ($60,000/year) for thirty years. You've taken in $1,800,000 according to our table, and you say to us that your net worth is about $400,000; the percent thus works out to be

$$\frac{\$400{,}000 \text{ (your net worth)}}{\$1{,}800{,}000 \text{ (your earnings after 20 years)}} \times 100\% = 22.2\%$$

which is very good! It's difficult (but not nearly impossible) to top 25 percent even after twenty years, give or take bonanzas made in the stock market or money married or inherited. You already know that I'm not about to push you into the stock market, but as for marrying or inheriting money, go for it!

HOW WEALTH IS CREATED

There are a million ways to spend money, but less than two handfuls of ways to create wealth. The principal ways you do it are:

1. By earning interest on money you invest (letting time make money for you)
2. By selling something for more than you paid for it (buy low–sell high, or letting your brilliance make money for you)
3. By inheriting wealth (letting the old parental units make money for you)
4. By combinations (marrying money)
5. By saving money on taxes (getting some or all of your withholding back and doing more brilliant things with it)

6. By receiving dividends (by letting corporations and other public and private organizations use your money to make money, at which time they generally give you some of it)
7. By gambling (letting pure dumb luck make money—unless you're a professional gambler)
8. By engaging in illegal activities (these generate the most wealth of all, but drug smugglers say South American jails are pure hell, and inside traders who get their pictures in the paper don't look as happy as I want you to)

This is a very short list, true, but that's about it. Most of what you will do in this book concerns numbers 1, 2, 5, and 6. I must point out, however, that I have no ideological objection to numbers 3 and 4. Just try to be gracious when it happens to you.

WHAT FORMS WEALTH TAKES

This is going to be a short book, guaranteed; therefore, we don't have enough room for a complete list. But an abbreviated list that will do nicely goes something like this:

- Old eyeglasses (these should be worth money but generally aren't)
- Cash in the bank (the poorest place for you, but best for your bank)
- Cash in the mattress (okay only if it fell out of your pocketbook)
- Pennies in jars (I know, you're going to roll them someday)
- Your house and the stuff in it (the part the mortgage company doesn't own)
- Stocks (only buy the ones that go up)
- Bonds (the U.S. government always pays theirs)
- Art or antiques (my wife, Charlotte, won't let me sell any, though)

- Your partnership share in a business (that $50 you invested in your brother-in-law's worm ranch)
- Mortgages you own on other folks' houses and such (let's hope they pay on time)
- Cars (but a new car never really adds to wealth, only to ego)
- Gold (but not what's in your teeth)
- Silver (six cents worth in a quarter, beats putting pennies in a jar)
- A tax refund coming (the check is in the mail)
- Houses, duplexes, apartments you own and rent (neat stuff until the tenants skip)
- Cash value of your life insurance (the awfulest investment of all)
- Mutual funds (stock investing for people who don't want to make it their career)
- Your clothing (all of it probably would bring $200 at a yard sale)
- An annuity (if this book sells, I should get a few dollars a year for some time to come)
- 243,189 other things that are worth money! (but someone besides you has to believe they are)

RISK AND RETURN: WHAT CHANCES WILL YOU TAKE?

We know some of the shapes and sizes that wealth comes in, and you know what wealth means to *you*. We've also noticed what a surprising amount of money we earn over ten, twenty-five, or fifty years. Even at the low end, $20,000, it adds up. What's missing?

Well, we haven't said much about what you're willing to do to make money on your money. Earlier I mentioned your "risk preferences" as a key ingredient in wealth creation. And, in passing, I mentioned Sue who still thinks any investment that offers more than a 5 1/4 percent return is too "risky." So Sue keeps her money in a passbook savings account—what about you? Ah, yours is in a money market fund—you high roller, you!

Since later in this book we'll talk about risk in connection with ways to create wealth, let's stop here to look at a picture and talk about the general idea of taking a risk to make money. The basic principle seems so obvious you'll laugh at my nerve for selling it (MBA students actually pay tuition to learn it). Every fool knows that:

> The bigger the chance you'll take, the more money you may win. Or lose.

So you're laughing, but you'd be surprised how many sensible people screw it up in practice and either (1) behave like every fool, or (2) do nothing (behave like an ostrich).

Look at Figure 1 and let's talk about some interpretations of it.

The straight line (labeled risk-return line) says that way up at the high end, for every "great deal" on which you expect to make a killing, there is also a high chance that you'll lose your shirt. A very small case in point: A graduate student of mine spent $404.32 of her student loan money on Monsanto stock options. She figured she could quadruple her money in four

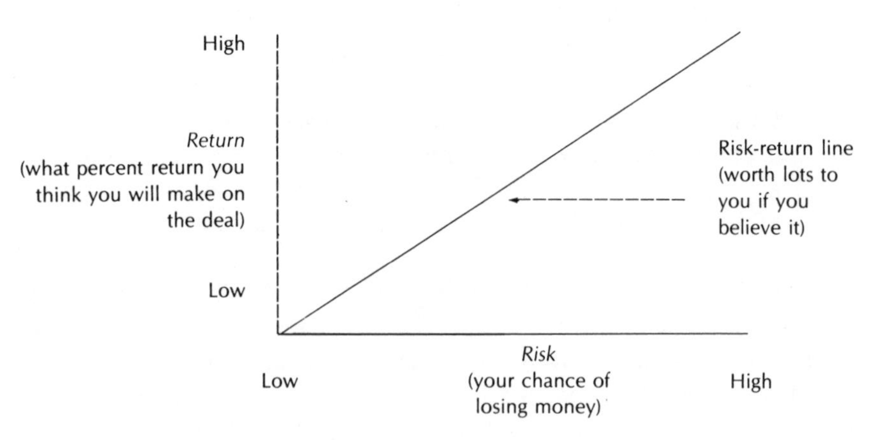

Figure 1

months. Instead, she lost every dime exactly $404.32. That's risk and return from the painful end, and two months rent back then.

Figure 1 also tells us that if you are willing to settle for low returns (stuff like keeping your money in a savings account), there is practically (not zero but practically) no chance you will lose it. Remember Sue and her 5 1/4 percent.

But all this is better explained if we redraw Figure 1 as Figure 2.

You can see that we've added four points, A, B, C, and D. A quick word about each of these in turn:

Point A: Tells us that if you are willing to settle for low returns you can earn these with low risk.

Point B: Tells us that if you go for high returns, you will run a high risk of losing your money.

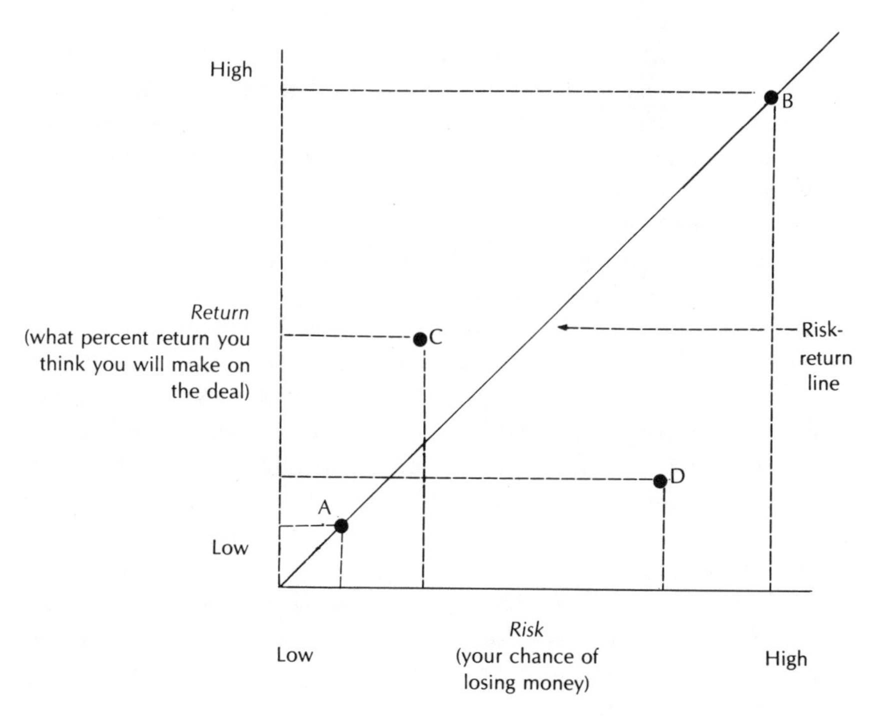

Figure 2

Point C: Tells us that if you *think* you are getting a high return with a low risk, you still believe in the tooth fairy

Point D: Tells us that if you accept a high risk to get a low return, one of three things is happening: (1) you are incredibly gullible, (2) you don't recognize risk when it's breathing in your face, or (3) you have the book turned upside down!

When someone shows you an investment and claims that the point relating risk and return is above the risk-return line (as in point C), call the sheriff. When you buy a deal in which the return is below the line, as in point D, call your shrink! (How do you tell how risky something is and whether the return is right? Keep reading!)

It's as simple as that: There really *is* no free lunch in America. Lots and lots of people sell free lunches, and lots of folks buy free lunches, and lots of folks franchise free lunches, and even more folks do the accounting, PR, and legal work for free-lunch producers. But there are absolutely, positively no free lunches. Trust me! Now do that homily in cross-stitch, hang it over your desk, and say it to yourself every day. You'd be amazed at what greed does to common sense.

Lots of things determine how much risk folks like you and me will accept to earn more money. Things such as our age, whether we have family obligations, whether we've been successful (or stung) before, the way we were brought up, our personality characteristics, whether we trust or distrust intangibles, and many more. We'll examine that idea in more detail in the next chapter. In the meantime, bear in mind that your risk preference can change during your life—in fact, *you* can change it. It has a lot to do with trying new things in a small way at first, building on successes, but not being traumatized by failures. So don't lose hope for Sue—she's young, but since she's smart she'll probably figure out how she can do a lot better than a passbook savings account without losing her shirt or asking Dad every time she makes a move.

RISK-TAKING—REPRISE

Back to the graduate student who fell off the risk-return line and lost her student loan money before the end of the semester. This same graduate student invested in photographs before coming to graduate school and getting so smart. Photographs are worse than stock options for risk—in general. But she chose well, and over the years she's been selling them—at ten times the price for which she bought them. She hasn't missed yet. So she went way out on the risk-return line and this time she didn't fall off. For taking a considerable risk, she's reaped a handsome reward.

What does that tell us? (1) It helps a lot to know what you're doing (she knew something about photographs but nothing about stock options), otherwise you might as well be playing the slot machines. (2) Everybody screws up sometime. You can look at the possibility of future failures as a valuable part of your education as a wealth-creating investor. Or you can look at possible failure as a reason *never* to take a risk and get in the game. Overwhelming fear of failure just is not part of the mindset you need to make money. But normal caution, knowing your own limits, and understanding risk are *always* appropriate before you take a risk. They *are* part of a wealth-creating mindset, the part that will keep your mistakes to a tolerable minimum as you amass the wealth you want.

DISCIPLINE: HOW TO LOSE FIFTY POUNDS

I remember a story about a traveling salesman who saw a farmer lifting a 2,000-pound cow. "How did you learn to perform such a feat?" he asked. "Easy," said the farmer, "when the calf was a day old, I started lifting it and I lifted it every day until right now." Now that smells of calf manure, but the implied moral is sound. *Discipline* (having the psychological mechanism that lets you order, control, and monitor your behavior) is a great thing—even if you're not into cow-lifting.

You've seen those ads, too, that promise you can lose fifty pounds if you will just give up your second cup of coffee every day. Yes, more manure, but again the implied lesson is a good one. Massive achievements, whatever they are, generally result from addition, not multiplication. It's adding up the calories of the desserts, candy, sugar, and beer you give up for six months that loses fifty pounds, not giving up *all* food for four weeks. It's lots of little individual gains added together that make miracles. The other kind of miracles are seen mostly in game shows, grocery-store romance novels, and get-rich-quick ads.

Creating wealth on a salary is much the same. To do it successfully, you must have discipline—and diligence (diligence is having discipline every single morning!). Addition is a powerful weapon. If you don't believe that, consider this: The average saving rate in the United States is a bit less than 5 percent of after-tax income. If you earn $35,000 a year and save 5 percent of your after-tax income, and you do this for forty years (typical earning period for most of us), and if this accumulates interest at just 7 percent, you'll have a little over a quarter of a million dollars at that time—just from saving. And the best thing about this deal is that you can burn this book and go fishing (if you start soon enough).

Without discipline and diligence, you'll never lose weight, you'll never accumulate much wealth on a salary, and you'll never learn to lift a 2,000-pound cow. On the other hand, with only a *little* discipline for a long enough time, look what you can do. Wonders.

PULLING THE TRIGGER

One of my favorite MBAs was named Vaughn. He had been one of the youngest infantry officers in Vietnam. After we taught Vaughn mindset and how to talk like a quant jock (a powerful combination) he became a CPA. Tiring of that very quickly, he started his own real estate development company and made quite a bit of money. (He lost quite a bit too.) I used to invite Vaughn back every spring to address the entrepreneurship class that I teach. He would assume the lotus position on the table in front of the class, and exhort fifty or so MBAs to learn to "pull the trigger" if they were ever to make a killing. Vaughn thought inability to pull the trigger (not being able to make that first all-important decision *to do it*) was the greatest impediment to successful entrepreneurship.

You may remember the first time you jumped off the diving board (the low one in my case), or your first public speech in high school, or your first date. Imagine the size of the trigger Columbus had to pull to sail west past the point where everyone knew the earth stopped. (Maybe it was easier for his crew. Queen Isabella reportedly told them one morning that they could get on the ship right then or rot in Spanish jails. Some choice!)

Fear of overcoming inertia (something the shrinks call hypengyophobia) may be stimulated by your thinking that any *really* bold stroke you take will cause instant fiscal disaster. Add up enough of these and you get a big pile of missed opportunities. It can work the other way too. Many folks stick with a stock on the way down, long after they should have bailed out. Immobility won't help you make your pile of dollars grow.

Sure, getting started on something new is tough. I spent two weeks putting it off and half a day staring at my Royal manual typewriter (with a clean sheet of paper in it) before I wrote a single word of this book. Hypengyophobia. My publisher knows this and keeps sending me notes assuring me that it will be a bestseller. See Dick's publisher lie. See Dick type faster.

However, to create wealth, you will have to pull the trigger. You can wait two weeks (like I did) or two months or two years, but one day you'll just get up and set the wheels in motion. Until that time, your total ($233) savings grow at 5 1/4 percent, the crew just rots in a Spanish jail, and America remains undiscovered!

Reasons why salaried people fail to create wealth include:

- Lack of money (a poor excuse if you're not on food stamps)
- Lack of discipline (sue your parents)
- Lack of enthusiasm (remember, being rich is more fun than being poor)
- Lack of knowledge about finance (in 13 more chapters we'll have cured that)

- Lack of knowledge about taxes and tax laws (Chapter 5 will push you in that direction)
- Procrastination (fancy word for not being able to pull the trigger)
- Lack of goals (that famous passage from *Alice in Wonderland*, about if you don't know where you want to be any road will take you there, is so overquoted that I'll spare you)
- Lack of sex (Woody Allen says this causes everything)

Reasons why salaried people *are* successful at creating wealth include:

- Being willing to pull the trigger
- Lack of sex (so if you're lying there alone, get out of bed and read the *Wall Street Journal*)

Upward and onward to Chapter 3!

3

How Much Are You In For and How to Boost the Ante

"Money is round. It rolls away."
SHOLEM ALEICHEM
"Thrift, thrift, Horatio!"
WILLIAM SHAKESPEARE

BUT YOU'VE GOT TO HAVE MONEY TO MAKE MONEY. AND I DON'T HAVE ANY MONEY

I guessed that when you bought the book! But don't feel guilty! It turns out that very few people earning a salary between $20,000 and $70,000 think that they really have any money to invest. It's not that they are poor, and it's not necessarily that they are wastrels; it's not because they don't think about it either. It's all the fault of an English economist named John Maynard Keynes.

Keynes thought up the intellectual underpinning of much of the deficit financing our presidents and Congress have become so fond of since the 1930s. Keynes developed an economic concept that he called "the propensity to consume." And there lies the root cause of the problem. The propensity to consume is defined as

$$\frac{\text{What you spend}}{\text{What you earn}}$$

which for centuries before Keynes most thinking folks believed could not and most assuredly *should* not rise above 100 percent. However, Keynes destroyed that quaint bit of Victorian economic discipline with his idea that it was okay for *countries* to spend more than they earned and to print money to make up the deficit. And so, fifty years later, we have a nation of folks with propensities to consume that are above 100 percent. (I bet you know some.) Enter finance companies.

Most of us "live up to our incomes"; we spend whatever we make. When times are good, we spend more; when times are bad, we spend more, too! The logic is unassailable. Very few folks in the world would experience trauma coming up with ways to spend *more* money; yet most people experience trauma at least monthly figuring up ways to spend *less*. And so with Keynes's blessing (he died a very wealthy person by the way), we keep our propensities to consume at or above 100 percent.

BUT NOBODY HAS ANY MONEY

I don't know anyone on a salary who has lots and lots of money lying around. I just don't! And if there *were* millions of these folks, who would buy this book? No, having money lying around is not what this book is about. You and I are interested in just two things: (1) creating more current investable money without perversion, theft, risk to our health, or immorality, and (2) investing that money in such a way that wealth (with minimum risk) is created over time. Those with bags and bags of money lying around would not be interested in this book. (On a list of things that interest *them*, the Internal Revenue Service and the Drug Enforcement Agency generally rank number one and number two.) We'll assume your middle name isn't Moneybags and go on from there. We're going to find some money—to save, not to spend.

BUT A DOLLAR A WEEK AIN'T SHIT (AS THEY ARE FOND OF SAYING IN TEXAS)

Don't you believe it! Suppose you are in our income bracket, $20,000 to $70,000 annually. And further assume (Keynes's writing was just full of these heady assumptions) that your propensity to consume is exactly 100 percent; you spend it all. Assume again (but don't worry for a few pages yet where I got this one from) that you could reduce your consumption just 5 percent (and, you quant jocks, that would make your propensity to consume 95 percent). Now if you are earning $30,000 annually, we have you saving 5 percent of your pretax income, or $1,500; and if you are earning $60,000 we have you saving $3,000 a year. Now, with one last (but fairly safe) assumption, let's put these savings away in something very nearly risk-free at 7 percent a year return. For the results of all this arithmetic, frugality, and legerdemain, look now at Table 2 on page 36. Here you can see what this paltry 5 percent of pretax income amounts to at several times in the future. Look at a couple of examples. At a $20,00 income (our lowest level), your savings are worth almost $200,000 in forty years (good at that point for purchasing Geritol and burial insurance), but even at just twenty-five years you'll have over $60,000. For the heavier hitters, say at a $60,000 income, 5 percent of pretax saved over thirty-five years is nearly $400,000—no paltry sum. Of course, we've left out income tax on the investment return (did you really think I'd forget that?), but there are several ways we'll use later to beat the IRS out of a good part of that—not to worry now. Besides, saving 5 percent ain't shit, and this time the Texans are right.

TWO CLEVER APPROACHES TO REDUCING YOUR PROPENSITY TO CONSUME

The first method involves two-step *logic.* Step 1, you sit down and persuade yourself (you are assumed to be a completely rational, intelligent person) that reducing what you spend by a bit is do-able, desirable, practical, and not injurious to your health. Step 2, you do it! Sure. Of all the folks I know, that will work with fewer than a third. The rest of us (me included) have spent years developing these clever, workable, explainable ways (read "rationalizations," which we think our friends will believe too) to beat logic.

That leaves two-thirds of the population. For us, I prescribe the second method, the RIF approach, something I learned in the Air Force thirty-three years ago. Back then, I was a young lieutenant working on a Ph.D. who thought he understood management (meaning of the entire last phrase = "stupid"). One day, my unit received an RIF (reduction in force) notice. Now a reduction in force was the Air Force's painless, quick, efficient, and legal way of getting rid of officers. You see, the commanding general of the United States Air Force didn't fly around the world to each unit and sit down with the commander and ask him in a

Table 2

Amount you will have if 5% of your pretax income is invested at a nearly risk-free 7% return for the years shown

Your income	15	20	25	30	35	40
$20,000	$25,129	$ 40,995	$ 63,249	$ 94,461	$138,737	$199,633
$30,000	37,694	61,493	94,874	141,692	207,356	299,453
$40,000	50,258	81,990	126,498	188,922	276,474	399,276
$50,000	62,823	102,488	158,123	236,153	345,593	499,088
$60,000	75,387	122,985	189,747	283,383	397,110	598,906
$70,000	87,952	143,483	221,372	330,614	483,830	698,723

nice participatory manner whether or not he might be able to do without an officer or two here and there. Hell no! The Pentagon simply sent out a notice that effective on such and such a day there would be 3 percent fewer Air Force officers in the world. And voila! On or before that day, it happened—thousands of officers were separated. This is called a centralized, nearly paperwork-free decision process with instantaneous local adjustment. Would it work today? Today, there would probably be 18,500 lawsuits, 43 strikes, 11 demonstrations, and maybe even a small bombing. Back then, an RIF was an RIF and that's all there was to it.

But what's that mean to us free-spending, rationalizing "logic defiers"? Just this: If we can't save it after we get our hands on it, then, by God, we won't let ourselves ever see it. We'll take it out before we get it, stash it away, and we'll learn to live on 95 percent of what we're used to. Cruel and unusual? No, it's not. Out of sight, out of mind. We'll hardly notice. Besides, if Queen Isabella hadn't used this method on Columbus's sailors, you and I would still be trading wampum. We agreed in the last chapter that we need discipline—just a little *every* day—so in a couple of pages we'll talk about that: how to RIF our rationalizations and come up with 5 percent investable income. But first, a reminder.

DON'T GIVE UP YOUR LIQUIDITY

Liquidity is one of the fancy terms you learn in business school. It doesn't mean the same thing as all wealth; rather it refers to the kind of wealth you can get your hands on in a hurry if you need to. For example, if Michele has a net worth of $1 million, but the money is equity in an apartment house (what it's worth less what she owes on it), then getting her hands on that million in a hurry might be quite difficult for Michele. Selling an apartment house, to convert equity into spendable cash, is not something you can generally do between breakfast and lunch. Thus, we would say that Michele is not liquid. Of course, she could borrow against the apartment house instead of selling it, but generally that's hard to do between breakfast and lunch too.

On the other hand, if you are worth, say, $250,000 and all of it is in the bank (U.S., not Swiss), then you are completely liquid, which means you can turn it all into "spendable cash" as fast as you can get to the bank. Makes a lot of difference, you see. Wealth can be liquid (the bank account) or illiquid (an apartment house). Most of us need *some* liquid wealth (or at least the ability to get our hands on some cash in a hurry). Let's see why and maybe even how much.

- *Transactions Needs*: This is another fancy phrase meaning cash you need to pay your daily, weekly, and monthly bills, money to buy lunch, pay the mortgage, get on the train, buy gas, purchase a newspaper, park your car, drop in a beggar's cup, buy a dress, or put in the football pool. Most of us charge a good bit of this (on credit cards, open charge accounts) with the anticipation that we will pay it when the bills come in at the end of the month. Regardless of *how* you handle it, you do need at least a month's worth of expenditures in cash or quick easy credit (cards will do). If you spend $3,000 a month, then you need about $3,000 in liquid funds.
- *Cessation of Earnings Needs:* These are not words that business school students like to talk about. At some point in your working life, you'll get fired, or quit voluntarily, just hang it up for a while, and say piss on it all. And as the saying goes, you'll "find yourself between opportunities." In any case, you'll need money to carry you through, the liquid kind. If you own an apartment house like Michele, and if you plan on using that money for these cessation-of-earnings needs, and you have to sell the apartment quickly, you probably will take a bath on the sale—fancy term for buy high–sell low. If you are rich, none of this matters. But for us salaried folks, we are talking about liquid wealth of about two to three months' expenditures. This can be in *any* form you can get your hands on quickly without taking a bath. This generally excludes diamonds, fine art, old rare stamps, your 1/1000th interest in an Alaska gold mine, and the antique chair your mother left you. The bottom line here is that if you invest your cessation of earnings money in something

that denies you liquidity, times will be extra tough during the "between opportunities" periods in your life. Yes, two to three months of liquid funds can be borrowed. But doing so right *after* you've lost your job makes for a weird-looking loan application, and bankers rarely have hearts, no matter what you learned in your anatomy course.

- *Unforeseen Needs:* There must be 11,235 of these—an extended sickness (anything over a month can and should be handled with medical insurance), a blown engine in your Z-car (about $4,500), your favorite cousin falls and breaks her leg and needs help, your house needs a new roof (after only six years and the contractor left town). Let's see, that leaves 11,231 needs to go! You know what I mean, all those unplannable vicissitudes in life that make planners look like idiots. How much do we need for unforeseen needs? For most of us right in the middle of the $20,000 to $70,000 range, this figure is about $10,000. Ten thousand dollars seems to cover just about any siege of bad luck we would likely encounter. Of course, if you are that character Al Capp used to draw who went around under a cloud of continuous bad luck, then you might need more. Your unforeseen needs can be handled with a bank line of credit, with cash in the bank (or under the mattress), savings, any near cash assets (CDs, money market accounts, or a rich parent). The best way to handle this is to have quick borrowing capacity (you call your banker and the money is in your checking account in one hour) for these needs. Yes, Virginia, this *can* and *is* done regardless of how you've been treated lately by your bank, but more on how to do that in a later chapter. Right now, I'm saying to you that if you earn $45,000 a year, you need to arrange *to have access to* at least $10,000 so you don't come apart in an emergency. That comes to about a fourth. Make sense?
- *Death Needs:* I know, this sounds macabre; business students won't even *think* about this one. But we all will go. If you have no children and no one will miss you when you go, then this amount needs to be only enough to bury (or cremate) you. Actually, the city you live in will do it free if you die a pauper, but such funerals are fairly shabby. Most

of us prefer to handle this need with life insurance (the cheap kind—term, of course). And that makes the best sense, too! Pay a few cents a day to handle the ultimate risk to those you leave behind. The rich always leave lots and lots of money behind so they can skip this paragraph. On the other hand, if you have eleven children, support your parents, owe on three cars and two houses, and are in arrears on all six of your credit cards, then you needs lots and lots of term insurance. And if this bleak scenario strongly suggests suicide, try to avoid it because most insurance policies won't pay off if you *are* successful in arranging your own departure. How much insurance you and I need to handle our death will be covered in excruciating detail in Chapter 13, so let's bag it for right now.

WHERE'S THAT LEAVE US?

Let's count up: a month's needs right at your fingertips, two to three months' expenditures available without selling something low that you bought high, about a fourth of your annual income that you can get your hands on fairly quickly for emergencies, and enough term insurance to handle the mess you leave behind if you go unexpectedly. Such would be a reasonable plan for liquidity. Don't get me wrong—liquidity *and* wealth can be the same thing. Cash is wealth and also very liquid (unless, of course, the mattress catches fire). However, they can be *entirely* different. Owning a house in Houston in which you have $20,000 equity and which you have had for sale for over a year without an offer is wealth, but most assuredly it is *not* liquidity—and that's what this book is all about!

LIVING IN YOUR OWN WEALTH

Sounds almost decadent, doesn't it? But that's what most of us do. Let's count up the assets we typically own that are used strictly for *living* instead of investing:

- *Your House or Condo*: I know, you could sell it tomorrow for $15,000 more than you paid for it, but remember if you do, you are out on the street, and whatever you buy will cost you more. I'm not against owning homes (quite the contrary, in fact) but I want you to realize that owning your home is primarily a family/comfort/lifestyle decision. A home is shelter. If you sell it, you put the family out on the street!
- *Your Car(s)*: I've said it once and I'll say it at least twice more before we get to the end of this book. There is *no* research that suggests that buying a car ever adds to your wealth, but *lots* of research that suggests it adds to your ego. (Lots of experience too—I *loved* that chopped and channeled 1932 Ford.) Most of us need a car for transportation; some of us need one for ego. But we all need to remember that buying one (or two or three) reduces our ability to create wealth, so we should weigh the benefits accordingly.
- *Your Clothes*: Nothing, but nothing, makes you feel as good as the first time you put on a really smashing dress. I don't know this from first-hand experience (my name is Dick, not Dorothy), but my wife Charlotte tells me it's so. There has also been a rash of books recently that claim that the quality of your wardrobe is directly related to your salary and organizational level in the company. I once was on a talk show with a guy who wrote one of those books and he looked like he shopped at the PTA thrift store. Fun, yes; ego boosters, yes; but wealth creators clothes aren't.
- *Your Knicknacks:* Neither a 46–foot Bertram yacht, a Piper Saratoga plane, a lifetime subscription to *National Geographic,* $20,000 worth of furniture, a $5,000 stereo, nor a Vitafit stationary home gymnasium adds one penny to your wealth. True, all of us like "knicknacks" and all of us need *some* (you heard right, all of us), but going over the hill on "knicknack spending" makes for a swinging pad and an empty bank account but *no* wealth creation. Have fun, but keep your eye on your wealth goal at the same time. As we said earlier, don't wait until you're 80 to buy a Porsche, but on the other hand don't make $2,500-a-month payments on a Bertram yacht when you're twenty-five and you earn $4,000 a month either! (Commercial fishermen excluded!)

SO WHERE'S THAT LEAVE US NOW?

Rule 1: Before you can do any serious wealth creation planning, you need to provide in an orderly way for the needs that life throws your way today and tomorrow. This is done with a combination of liquid assets, credit, and term insurance, without injury to life, limb, or ego. *Rule 2:* You are sitting in the middle of a lot of what you are worth. Creature comforts cost money, and, let's face it, many of them are not investments in anything but a higher standard of living and an elevated ego—which are themselves not bad if they are served *in* your wealth creation plan, not at the expense of it. So on to "how."

RAISING THE ANTE: HELP FROM COLUMNS AND ROWS

My brother, Bob, is the consummate budgeter. During his professional career, he was V.P. Manufacturing for a lingerie company and mastered industrial budgeting. But for many years his personal propensity to consume fluctuated right around 101 percent, so he was "forced" into personal budgeting as a survival strategy. Anyway, he's learned it well from both sides, so I listen to him. (I also listen to him when he talks about fishing.)

You and I are interested in budgeting as a way to raise the ante—a way to arrange our month-to-month finances so that when the month ends, we have *more* to invest than we do now. Other than for that one worthy purpose, I say that budgeting is right down there next to taking unflavored cod-liver oil as something we really *want* to do. Now some lucky people have built-in budgeting systems, something in their genetic makeup that keeps outgo less than income without their putting it down on paper. The rest of us generally benefit from a simple budgeting exercise once in a while, and that's what we want to do now. But remember, our purpose is to "raise the ante," not just fill space with numbers. Oh yes, we called this section "Help from Columns and Rows." For those readers who have not taken matrix algebra (clearly the sane ones), columns go up and down and rows go from left to right.

Basically, budgeting is a way to keep outgo in line with income. Many people do it with calories to lose weight; lots more do it successfully with money. To begin, collect:

- Your checks or check register from last year
- A list of sources and amounts of all your income last year
- A list of anything you paid with cash (i.e., anything that was legal)
- Other useful stuff (Swiss bank account records, poker winnings, your tax return, and old Statue of Liberty tickets)

Get these in some kind of orderly arrangement (by month, by category of income, by category of expenses), and take these with several pencils and your calculator or computer to a quiet place for a couple of hours' work.

Figure out your monthly income by dividing your total

yearly income by 12, then do the same thing with your expenses. Some of your expenses will be paid monthly (rent or mortgage payment, gas for the car, food, and the like). Others will be paid yearly (insurance premiums, property taxes, protection paid to the neighborhood rowdies, and income taxes beyond what was withheld; if your income taxes are being paid quarterly, you'll have to divide by 3 to get them back into a monthly amount—which means maybe you *should* have taken matrix algebra after all). Still with us?

At this point, as you look at your budgeted monthly income and your budgeted monthly expenses, here are the possible outcomes:

Outcome	Interpretation
1. Your monthly income is several times your monthly expenses.	Either you are rich and have forgotten that fact or you have misplaced a decimal point somewhere.
2. Your monthly expenses are several times your monthly income	Neither I nor anyone else can help you at this point. Bankruptcy is near. Either that or you dropped a decimal point.
3. Your monthly expenses are less than your monthly income but you never have any money left over.	Either you can't add correctly, or several hundred dollars a month are disappearing down a rat hole called "miscellaneous expenses" that you forgot to count.
4. Your monthly expenses are less than your monthly income and you *do* have money left over at the end of the month.	Congratulations! You took matrix algebra and forgot to tell us, or you know my brother, Bob.
5. Your monthly income is exactly equal to your monthly expenses.	You are probably lying!
6. You cannot get a total for either income or expenses.	Take matrix algebra, or *stop* drinking whatever it is you have in front of you.

Most of us fall into outcome 3 or 4. In either case, the budget format on pages 46–47 will help. If it's 3, it will help you find "miscellaneous expenses" because I've tried to list as many of them as I can think of. If it's 4, it will help you examine *all* of your expenses so that you can reduce some of them further if you want to save more. And if you just like columns and rows, it will be fun to do, but remember what happened to Bob Cratchit!

First, fill in column 2 with the total monthly amount you spend for each of the forty-five categories of expenses. Then go back, row by row, and divide the total monthly amount into *two* parts. Part 1 goes in column 3 (sounds like instructions for assembling a model airplane, doesn't it?) and represents the portion of what you spend that is sacrosanct, absolutely *cannot* be cut. Part 2 goes in column 4 and represents the portion of what you spend in each category that *could* (not *will*, mind you, but *could*) be cut out at least some. Be honest, forthcoming, candid, trustworthy, loyal, brave, clean, and reverent. But most of all, be honest!

Now look at the entries you have in column 4. These are your "action items"; this is where budgeting effort will pay off. After all, if you have a $900 per month mortgage payment in column 1, why bedevil yourself right now trying to reduce it. Don't make yourself neurotic. Worry about what you *can* control. Work on the amounts you put in column 4; this is where the action is, and this is where you will win if it's possible.

Total up column 4. That is your maximum possible monthly expense reduction—not what you'll actually reduce expenses by, but the *most* you can reduce expenses by. Most of us will come out actually cutting only a part of column 4, but a part is what we are after.

Now go back row by row and look closely at column 4. In each instance, make a decision about *how much you will cut*, and put this amount in column 5. These amounts represent your budgeting pact with yourself. They stand for your personal commitment to cut, your deal with the monetary devil. If the honest entry is zero, put it there. If you know you can cut, estimate how much and put that there.

Now total up column 5. This is your estimated monthly expenditure cut. If the total is zero, go back to page 27 and read it

COLUMN 1 Expense Item (in no particular order)	COLUMN 2 What I spend monthly on this item	COLUMN 3 What part of column 2 *cannot* be cut	COLUMN 4 What part of column 2 *could* be cut	COLUMN 5 Amount I agree to cut monthly
1. Rent or mortgage				
2. Electricity				
3. Telephone				
4. Water				
5. Cable television				
6. Fuel oil/gas				
7. House insurance				
8. Car insurance				
9. Health insurance				
10. Life insurance				
11. Lawn care				
12. Cleaning/housekeeper				
13. Trash pickup				
14. Subscriptions				
15. Pet food and care				
16. Food and foodstore items				
17. Booze				
18. Clothing				
19. Laundry–dry cleaning				
20. Gifts				
21. Entertainment/sports				

22. Vacation
23. House repair
24. Car repair
25. Car gas/oil/license
26. Commuting—train, bus
27. Furniture/appliances bought
28. Property taxes
29. Income taxes (federal/state)
30. Loan repayments
31. Haircut/beauty shop
32. Kids' allowances
33. Piano lessons (violins, too)
34. Summer camp
35. School/college tuition
36. School room/board/expenses
37. Doctor
38. Dentist
39. Lawyer
40. Veterinarian
41. Drugs (the legal kind)
42. Contributions
43. Pledges (church/synagogue)
44. Alimony (pay, not get)
45. Miscellaneous (God will get you if this is more than 2 percent of your total expenditures)

sober. For most people, this seemingly mindless exercise in columns and rows turns out to illuminate chances, not necessarily change behavior. But demonstrated chances to reduce expenses are the stuff that budgeting is made of. Go for it!

MY COLUMN 5 TOTAL IS ZERO, YOU SAY

Bullshit! You are more honest than that. My two cousins from Baltimore, Sandy and Brieta, took half a day of their visit with Charlotte and me at the beach to do the following little exercise. I asked them to make a list of ways to cut expenses that made sense for them on their income. And I limited them to half a day (which with time out for coffee, questions, bathroom, telephone, and miscellaneous came to three hours). Here is what they gave me:

111 PAINLESS WAYS TO SAVE MONEY
(Courtesy of my cousins Brieta and Sandy)

1. Use a less expensive phone service (MCI, Sprint, etc.)
2. Make phone calls after 5 and 11 P.M. when rates are lower.
3. Use limited phone service if available (maximum number of calls/month for *much* lower rates).
4. Buy a bunch of stamped postal cards and write occasionally instead of calling.
5. Use a low-priced (budget) rent-a-car service.
6. If you live in a city where garaging and taxes are very high, sell your car and use a budget rent-a-car service on weekends.
7. Pump your own gas.
8. Wash your own car or use the car wash on cheap days.
9. Carpool to work.
10. Carpool for kids' activities.
11. Fix/paint/don't trade your car for another year.
12. Consider bicycling to work occasionally on pretty days.
13. Change your own oil in your car.

14. Raise the deductible on your car insurance.
15. Raise the deductible on your homeowner's insurance.
16. Raise the deductible on your health insurance.
17. Raise the deductible on your blanket liability insurance.
18. Buy term insurance, not cash value.
19. Buy food specials.
20. Never shop when you're hungry.
21. Use food coupons religiously.
22. Swap food coupons with friends.
23. Subscribe to the Sunday paper only (it has the food coupons).
24. Buy generic food items.
25. Buy generic drugs.
26. Buy generic cigarettes.
27. Minimize your purchase of nonfood grocery store items.
28. Pick some of your own fruits and vegetables at a pick-your-own farm.
29. Consider joining a food coop.
30. Drink water as your major beverage instead of sodas.
31. Bag your lunch occasionally (especially with leftovers).
32. Wash and reuse tin foil at least once.
33. Start a small garden.
34. Cook in large quantities for more than one meal.
35. Buy discount vitamins.
36. Buy books at used book stores.
37. Swap paperback books with friends.
38. Buy good jug wine.
39. Feed your pets dry food. Dogs and cats thrive on dry food (only owners don't).
40. Substitute a picnic at an interesting place for eating out occasionally.
41. Substitute potluck dinners for entertainment occasionally.
42. Use only special airfare deals for vacation travel and plan far enough ahead to get them.

43. Camp out to avoid motel bills on vacation.
44. Visit relatives on vacation trips to save on motel bills.
45. Swap houses with other owners to save motel/hotel bills.
46. Shop around for the best buy in film development.
47. Shop around for dry-cleaning specials.
48. Use the laundromat dry-cleaning machines.
49. Get books from the public library instead of buying them.
50. Ask your doctor for sample drugs that she gets.
51. Reduce the number of your magazine subscriptions.
52. Quit insuring your kids (life, not health).
53. Rent video movies and invite friends to share the cost, avoiding ticket prices and maybe babysitters too.
54. Trade the professional service you render for a professional service you need.
55. Check the newspaper for free concerts, movies, and sporting events.
56. Reduce the number of hair-styling/barber shop visits.
57. Have a basement/garage sale at least every three years.
58. Sell unneeded items to second-hand shops.
59. Buy clothes on sale only.
60. Change buttons and belts to enhance your wardrobe.
61. Buy furniture only on sale or from discount stores.
62. Buy day-old bakery goods.
63. Exchange clothes with friends.
64. Use hand-me-downs for kids.
65. Use electricity in nonpeak hours.
66. Repair all water leaks immediately.
67. Buy more wash-and-wear clothes to save on dry-cleaning bills.
68. Save wrapping paper and ribbon for reuse.
69. Find free parking on the street and walk a few blocks.
70. Save grocery bags and use them for garbage bags.
71. Save and use plastic containers for freezer/refrigerator storage.

72. Buy rebate items and use the coupons.
73. Take in a roommate if you own or rent a house or apartment.
74. If you own the house and take in a roommate, take depreciation on the half of the house he or she uses.
75. See movies during early hour specials.
76. Exchange baby sitting hours with neighbors.
77. Take advantage of all senior citizen discounts (only if you qualify, of course!).
78. Buy monthly tokens/passes for buses/trains.
79. Make some of your own clothing.
80. Recycle old newspapers, bottles, and cans for money.
81. Paint your own house or employ your kids to do it.
82. Hide twenty-five percent of your children's toys and bring them out a year later as new toys.
83. Turn off your lights when you don't need them.
84. Reduce the wattage in 50 percent of your bulbs.
85. Turn down the thermostat at night.
86. Save up dishes in the dishwasher for two to three days.
87. Wash clothes only in cold water.
88. Consider joining an HMO.
89. Pay off your credit card on time to eliminate interest but not one day early.
90. Check out your credit union for interest charges on loans.
91. Turn up your air-conditioning thermostat two degrees.
92. Borrow from your bank or credit union to refinance expensive consumer loans.
93. Refinance your home mortgage if interest rates fall.
94. Put your kids to work on Saturdays.
95. Consider borrowing a wedding gown.
96. Increase the number of your withholding deductions.
97. Buy cheap Polaroid sunglasses; they work as well as expensive ones.
98. Have business cards printed to get commercial hotel or motel rates.

99. Postpone purchases for a while to save credit card/credit account interest.
100. Sell your ex-significant other's cross-country skis that are gathering dust in the attic.
101. Use discount car gas.
102. Quit smoking.
103. Give away one or more of your pets (after careful consideration). (Four dogs are really too many!)
104. Make—don't buy—clever gifts for friends/relatives.
105. Authorize your employer to withhold $100 a month from your pay and deposit it direct into a savings account.
106. Drop collision insurance on your car when it is four years old.
107. Consider going from a homeowner's insurance policy 5 down to a 3 or 2.
108. Make up a pantry inventory list so you won't double-buy and tie up money in food inventory; use shallow shelves so you can see what you've got. (Four cans of water chestnuts are too many!)
109. Use the YMCA instead of a more expensive fitness facility.
110. Walk four miles a day instead of using the YMCA.
111. Never pay for sex.

SOME HELPFUL IDEAS IN BUDGETING

- Always be flexible and leave room for unforeseen purchases/expenses.
- Don't lie to yourself.
- Don't commit to a budget that your psyche won't let you adhere to.
- Start with small "cuts" so you can win from the beginning.
- Get your spouse or significant other involved.
- Get your kids involved when they are old enough (puberty).
- Do this exercise (all five columns) at least once a year.

- Don't count on income increases to balance your budget—stick with expenses.

REPRISE

"I don't have enough money to invest" is a poor excuse. For all but a small handful of overcommitted (or just plain unlucky) readers, having money to invest is a simple but sometimes painful process of examining your financial behavior (as we've done here) and deciding what part of that behavior can and should change—for reasons that make sense to *you!* Remember, all you have to uncover in five columns is five percent of your pretax income to wind up with some real wealth. And that's a *lot* easier than matrix algebra. Onward!

4

Becoming a Quant Jock in Five Easy Steps

The more you get, the more you get.
TOM PETTY

What's a Quant Jock?

If this were a book about sex therapy, you'd have to try the advice a few times, wouldn't you? And if the book were about flying airplanes, you'd still have to "take the wheel" in the air to feel exactly what flying is all about. Well, guess what? This is a book about financial matters, and the joy of wealth means that you've got to become moderately comfortable with the "numbers" and numerical processes involved in measuring, estimating, figuring, counting, and ciphering up *wealth*. Take heart—doing the numbers might turn out like sex and flying, where getting there is more than half the fun. Don't glorify the end and despise the means!

In MBA programs, we call those men and women who demonstrate great facility with numbers "quant jocks." Quant jocks love to crunch numbers. Many never accumulate any real wealth in their professional careers, though. Just as reading about sex is quite different from doing it, being able to cipher up all the columns and rows of numbers is a lot different from making the decisions necessary to accumulate some real wealth. And in wealth creation, it's only numbers until (as Vaughn said) you pull the trigger and make it happen. Some quant jocks have the desire and guts necessary to accumulate real wealth. Others like to talk about, think about, write about, dream about, and even give talks about numbers. But they never get into bed with them.

BUT I DON'T HAVE A PC

It doesn't matter! In fact, without one you probably saved a couple thousand bucks you can invest wisely. I'll give you all of the tables you need right here in the book to figure things such as:

	Answer
• What one dollar saved and invested each week will accumulate to in ten years	Not much
• How much a week I have to save to have a $1,000,000 in five years	All you make plus $1,000 more a week
• How long it will take for my money to double	Depends on what rate of interest you're getting, of course
• How long my nestegg will last if I spend not only the interest but part of the principal too	Not as long as it would if you didn't
• How much I need to save a day to retire in 80 years on $100 a week	About 1¢

PCs are nice; they *do* solve a wide variety of problems, and if you have one and use it, so much the better. But they are not necessary for wealth creation; the answers they give are no more accurate than the tables I'll show you in this book, and for folks in the $20,000–$70,000 income range, we can do very nicely without one. We will, of course, have to become comfortable with using financial tables, but compared to flying upside down without instruments in a blizzard, financial tables are a snap. You'll love them!

THE MIRACLE OF COMPOUND INTEREST

This is a key concept, but if it's too elementary for you, move on (or back) right now to the first paragraph you don't understand. I'll assume that most of you are non-quant jocks and proceed accordingly. Let's start with a simple example. Suppose you put $100 in a savings account, which gives you 10 percent interest "compounded annually" (a totally unrealistic rate for a bank, but it makes the calculations easy). What happens:

The first day	Nothing, except the bank now has $100 of your money to lend to someone else and charge them for it.
At the end of the first year	Your savings account is now $110 . . . composed of your original $100 plus $10 interest the bank paid you.
At the end of the second year	Your savings account is now $121 composed of: • your original $100, plus • your first year interest of $10, plus • your second year interest of $11 calculated as: 10% × what you had in the bank at the end of the first year ($110), which is 10% × $110 = $11
At the end of the third year	That's too long to keep money in a savings account.

CAN'T I DO BETTER THAN THAT, COACH?

Sure you can. Pick up the newspaper and look for the first bank that offers you "quarterly compounding"—better yet, "daily compounding." What does that mean? I'll show you an example with quarterly compounding since that involves only four calculations. (Daily compounding works the same—just 365 calculations instead of four.)

Your new bank offers the same 10 percent interest but compounds it quarterly. Here's how it works:

The first day	They still have your $100
3 months later	Your savings account is now $102.50 calculated: • your original $100, plus • 10% interest on $100 for 3 months (1/4 of a year) 10% × $100 × 1/4 = $2.50
6 months later	Your savings account is now $105.06 calculated: • your original $100, plus • the $2.50 interest you earned the first quarter, plus • interest you earned the second quarter calculated: 10% × $102.50 × 1/4 (of a year) = $2.56

The savings account balance at the end of nine and twelve months would be figured in the same way. At the end of each quarter, the bank pays you interest on what was there during that quarter (including the interest you earned during the last quarter). The result at the end of the first year with quarterly compounding would be that your savings account balance is $110.39 instead of just $110.

Big deal, you say, what difference is 39 cents? Look at it this way. It's free money, and it's 0.39% a year more earned on your money! It's spendable! How can you find the bank that offers the best "compounding" deal? Simple, look for the one that says "daily compounding." (Bank competition is not yet at the point where anyone is offering hourly compounding.) If your bank doesn't say anything about the way they compound, they are probably screwing you (and without reading the sex book either)!

ISN'T THERE A BETTER WAY THAN DOING ALL THESE SILLY CALCULATIONS?

Of course, but I wanted you to know that you *could* do the calculations by hand. Otherwise, you would have to accept the tables as an article of faith and that's bad learning! Once upon a time long ago and far away, a smart person (a quant jock for sure) worked out compound interest tables to avoid doing all those tedious calculations, just as we just did, each time. In fact, the quant jock worked out different tables for different situations, so we'll take them one at a time, learn what each does and how to make it work for us. (Those of you with PCs or fairly sophisticated hand-held calculators can skip this part, but if you do you may never understand what goes on inside the black box. So consider plodding along with us.)

WHAT'S A DOLLAR WORTH LATER IF I LEAVE IT ALONE?

For starters, let's consider a situation in which someone puts a certain number of dollars in an investment, which pays a certain rate of interest compounded annually, and just leaves it there for a while. To figure out what it will be worth at any time in the future, look at Table 3 on pages 62–63.

Suppose you put $1,000 in an investment that offers 8 percent interest compounded annually and leave it there for ten years. What's it worth then? In Table 3, come down the years column (the leftmost column) to the ten-year row (remember columns go up and down, rows go from left to right). Go to the right on the ten-year row until you're under the 8% column where you'll find the value 2.1589. What's that value mean? That's what *one* dollar earning 8 percent would be worth in 10 years, so $1,000 would be worth $1,000 × 2.1589 = $2,158.90, not a bad haul.

It's really just that easy to use Table 3. Let's do a few more exercises just to make sure. Suppose this time you invest $7,500 at 10 percent for thirteen years. What's that worth? Same routine

Table 3

Dollar Principal Compounded Annually

End of Year	6%	8%	10%	12%	15%
1	$ 1.0600	$ 1.0800	$ 1.1000	$ 1.1200	$ 1.1500
2	1.1236	1.1664	1.2100	1.2544	1.1322
3	1.1910	1.2597	1.3310	1.4049	1.5209
4	1.2625	1.3605	1.4641	1.5735	1.7490
5	1.3382	1.4693	1.6105	1.7623	2.0114
6	1.4185	1.5869	1.7716	1.9738	2.3131
7	1.5036	1.7138	1.9487	2.2107	2.6600
8	1.5938	1.8509	2.1436	2.4760	3.0590
9	1.6895	1.9990	2.3579	2.7731	3.5179
10	1.7908	2.1589	2.5937	3.1058	4.0456
11	1.8983	2.3316	2.8531	3.4785	4.6524
12	2.0122	2.5182	3.1384	3.8960	5.3503
13	2.1329	2.7196	3.4523	4.3635	6.1528
14	2.2609	2.9372	3.7975	4.8871	7.0757
15	2.3966	3.1722	4.1772	5.4736	8.1371
16	2.5404	3.4259	4.5950	6.1304	9.3576
17	2.6928	3.7000	5.0545	6.8660	10.7613

18	2.8543	3.9960	5.5599	7.6900	12.3755
19	3.0256	4.3157	6.1159	8.6128	14.2318
20	3.2071	4.6610	6.7275	9.6463	16.3665
21	3.3996	5.0338	7.4002	10.8038	18.8215
22	3.6035	5.4365	8.1403	12.1003	21.6447
23	3.8197	5.8715	8.9543	13.5523	24.8915
24	4.0489	6.3412	9.8497	15.1786	28.6252
25	4.2919	6.8485	10.8347	17.0001	32.9190
26	4.5494	7.3964	11.9182	19.0401	37.8568
27	4.8223	7.9881	13.1100	21.3249	43.5353
28	5.1117	8.6271	14.4210	23.8839	50.0656
29	5.4184	9.3173	15.8631	26.7499	57.5755
30	5.7435	10.0627	17.4494	29.9599	66.2218
31	6.0881	10.8677	19.1943	33.5551	76.1435
32	6.4534	11.7371	21.1138	37.5817	87.5651
33	6.8406	12.6760	23.2252	42.0915	100.6998
34	7.2510	13.6901	25.5477	47.1425	115.8048
35	7.6861	14.7853	28.1024	52.7996	133.1755
36	8.1473	15.9682	30.9127	59.1356	153.1519
37	8.6361	17.2456	34.0039	66.2318	176.1246
38	9.1543	18.6253	37.4043	74.1797	202.5433
39	9.7035	20.1153	41.1448	83.0812	232.9248
40	10.2857	21.7245	45.2593	93.0510	267.8635

. . . go down the leftmost column to thirteen years, then out that row to 10 percent where we find 3.4523 (the value of one dollar at that point in time). Then $7,500 × 3.4523 = $25,892.25, a tidy sum (but unless you like multiplying by hand, we had to use a calculator to do the arithmetic that time).

One more, but a bit more complicated this time. You put $5,000 in an investment worth 12 percent for nine years. At the end of six years, the investment return falls to 8 percent for the remaining three years. What will it be worth at the end of the nine years? This is what they call a "two-stepper."

Step 1 Let's figure what the investment is worth at the end of six years: Same routine, in the table, down the leftmost column to the six-year row, out that row to the 12 percent column where we find the value 1.9738. Multiply $5,000 × 1.9738 and get the answer $9869.00.

Step 2 Let's now see what $9,869 is worth in three years (the period that remains) at 8 percent. The right value this time is 1.2597 (did you get it?), which when multiplied by $9,869 is $9,869 × 1.2597 = $12,431.98, the answer to our problem. Simple as that.

WHAT'S A DOLLAR A YEAR WORTH FOR SEVERAL YEARS IF I LEAVE IT ALONE?

Ah, a different deal this time. Before, we made a *one-shot* investment. Now we are talking about situations where people put in a fixed amount *each year* for a number of years and let the whole thing (principal plus interest) compound. To solve these kinds of problems we use Table 4.

Suppose you put $2,000 *a year* in an investment which yields 10 percent interest compounded annually. What's it worth at the end of eighteen years? Go down the leftmost column of Table 4 to the eighteen-year row, then out that row to the 10 percent column where we find the value 50.1591. That's what one dollar a year would be worth at 10 percent after eighteen years. So the answer to our problem is $2,000 × 50.1591 = $100,318.20. If you put in $36,000, you will get out $100,318—is this fun, or what?

Now let's do a bit of a brain teaser. This time, you put $3,500 a year in an 8 percent investment for thirteen years; then you increase your annual deposit to $5,000 for five more years while the whole thing yields 12 percent. What's all that worth then? (*Hint:* A lot!) Okay, we've got a "four-stepper" this time.

Step 1 Look in Table 4 for thirteen years at 8 percent, where you should find the value 23.2149. Multiply that by $3,500 to get $81,252.15, which is what your investment is worth at the end of 13 years.

Step 2 Now your $81,252.15 will sit there and earn 12% (while you put in $5,000 a year for five more years), so let's see first what just your $81,252.15 will be worth five years from now. Since you're not going to add more to it, go back and use Table 3. Look at the 12 percent row for five years and you will see 1.7623. Then multiply $81,252.15 × 1.7623 to get $143,190.66. Just hang on to this answer for a minute.

Step 3 For the last five years you plan to invest $5,000 *a year* at 12 percent, so it's back to Table 4. Quick—down the leftmost column to the five-year row, out that row to the 12 percent column, and you'll find 7.1152. Multiplying this by $5,000, we get $5,000 × 7.1152 = $35,576. Hold on to this answer for another second please.

Step 4 Add together the result of steps 2 and 3—$143,190.66 + $35,576 = $178,766.66—and there it is to the penny!

It just doesn't get more complicated than that, folks! If you can follow those four steps and if they make sense to you, you qualify for a third-class quant jock merit badge.

Table 4

One Dollar per Annum Compounded Annually

End of Year	6%	8%	10%	12%	15%
1	$ 1.0600	$ 1.0800	$ 1.1000	$ 1.1200	$ 1.1500
2	2.1836	2.2464	2.3100	2.3744	2.4725
3	3.3746	3.5061	3.6410	3.7793	3.9934
4	4.6371	4.8666	5.1051	5.3528	5.7424
5	5.9753	6.3359	6.7156	7.1152	7.7537
6	7.3938	7.9228	8.4872	9.0890	10.0668
7	8.8975	9.6366	10.4359	11.2297	12.7268
8	10.4913	11.4876	12.5795	13.7757	15.7858
9	12.1808	13.4866	14.3974	16.5487	19.3037
10	13.9716	15.6455	17.5312	19.6546	23.3493
11	15.8699	17.9771	20.3843	23.1331	28.0017
12	17.8821	20.4953	23.5227	27.0291	33.3519
13	20.0151	23.2149	26.9750	31.3926	39.5047
14	22.2760	26.1521	30.7725	36.2797	46.5804
15	24.6725	29.3243	34.9497	41.7533	54.7175
16	27.2129	32.7502	39.5447	47.8837	64.0751
17	29.9057	36.4502	44.5992	54.7497	74.8364

18	32.7600	40.4463	50.1591	62.4397	87.2118
19	35.7856	44.7620	56.2750	71.0524	101.4436
20	38.9927	49.4229	63.0025	80.6987	117.8101
21	42.3923	54.4568	70.4027	91.5026	136.6316
22	45.9958	59.8933	78.5430	103.6029	158.2764
23	49.8156	65.7648	87.4973	117.1552	183.1678
24	53.8645	72.1059	97.3471	132.3339	211.7930
25	58.1564	78.9544	108.1818	149.3339	244.7120
26	62.7058	86.3508	120.0999	168.3740	282.5688
27	67.5281	94.3388	133.2099	189.6989	326.1041
28	72.6398	102.9659	147.6309	213.5828	376.1697
29	78.0582	112.2832	163.4940	240.3327	433.7451
30	83.8017	122.3459	180.9434	270.2926	499.9569
31	89.8898	133.2135	200.1378	303.8477	576.1005
32	96.3432	144.9506	221.2515	341.4294	663.6655
33	103.1838	157.6267	244.4767	383.5210	764.3654
34	110.4348	171.3168	270.0244	430.6635	880.1702
35	118.1209	186.1021	298.1268	483.4631	1013.3757
36	126.2681	202.0703	329.0395	542.5987	1166.4975
37	134.9042	219.3158	363.0434	608.8305	1342.6222
38	144.0585	237.9412	400.4478	683.0102	1545.1655
39	153.7620	258.0565	441.5926	766.0914	1778.0903
40	164.0477	279.7810	486.8518	859.1424	2045.9539

BUT CAN ALL THIS HELP ME BECOME A MILLIONAIRE?

Fair question. Let's put some of our "table work" to work for us figuring out exactly what it takes to accumulate certain amounts of wealth. After all, your wealth creation is what this book is all about. Since there's a mystique about becoming a millionaire, let's use that wealth level, $1 million, in an example or two.

Accumulating wealth (as we have seen in those table problems we just worked) is a function of:

- How much money you start with (or can put away each year)
- What rates of interest it earns (generally called yield)
- How long you keep it invested

The magic that comes from compounding money year after year means little if you are putting away $100 a year—or for that matter, if the investment yields 2 percent a year or, if you only stay

at it a year or two. But wealth mounts up rapidly when you (1) invest a reasonable sum each year, (2) your investment(s) earns reasonable yields, and (3) you stick with it. To prove this to yourself, look back at Table 3. There you can see (in the forty-year row under the 15 percent column) that a single dollar invested for forty years at 15 percent will then be worth $267.86. That's quite a sum, all from only one original dollar. If you started with $1,000 instead of only $1.00, and if you left it there compounding at 15 percent for forty years, then you already know that we'd calculate the answer as $1,000 × 267.87 = $267,860, quite a wad. We should all be so lucky!

The effect of consistently adding to your investment is shown by referring to Table 4 again. Look at the forty-year row under the 15 percent column, where you'll see 2045.95, which is what $1.00 invested *each year* at 15% for forty years would be worth then—over $2,000 from only a dollar *a year*.

But let's say you want to accumulate $1 million. Great, we'll use Table 4 to help us think through your goal. After all, if you are 67 years old and can afford to invest only $50 a week and the best investment yield you can get is 6 percent, you will be about 145 years old when you reach your goal, and only Methuselah and a few old Russians eating yogurt claim to have lived that long. On the other hand, if you are in your twenties and can put away several thousand a year with a good yield, a million-dollar wealth may be quite reasonable. So, the first thing we always ought to do is to test the *reasonableness* of our wealth goal. Can we reach it? Will we live long enough? Can we invest enough each year to make it? And will our yield be high enough to make it come true?

You, then, start with your age (28 it is). Then decide when you want to have your million accumulated (by age 60). So 60 − 28 = 32 years! Go immediately to the 32-year row in Table 4; nothing else matters (unless you lied about your age). Only the five numbers on that row make any sense to your situation. Let's set these five numbers out (as they say in publishing):

	6%	8%	10%	12%	15%
32 years	96.3432	144.9506	221.2515	341.4294	663.6655

Remember, each of these numbers represents what $1.00 invested *each year* will be worth at the indicated percent yields. Think now about what yield you can expect to earn. (Recall the discussion in Chapter 2 about risk, return, the tooth fairy, and honesty.) Let's say that when you have thought it over you've decided that for the risk you are willing to take you can probably expect to earn an investment yield of 8 percent. Safe, but respectable!

This now means that only the number under 8 percent has meaning for *your* situation, so let's discard all the others and set out what's left:

	8%
32 years	144.9506

This means that for a 28-year-old person who expects to earn an investment yield of 8 percent, the total of $1.00 invested per year with interest will be $144.95 by the time you are sixty years old. So if you want $1 million thirty-two years from now, the correct calculation to find the amount you need to invest *every year* is:

$$\frac{\$1{,}000{,}000}{144.95} = \$6{,}898.93$$

You might think, there is no way I can possibly afford to invest nearly $6,900 every year. Fine, I say. Folks will still love you, but you won't accumulate $1 million in wealth by the time you are sixty! At this point, there are four things you can do:

- Lie about your present age.
- Extend the time in which you want to accumulate this wealth.
- Play tooth fairy games about the investment yield you will earn.
- Set a more appropriate wealth goal.

Only suggestions 2 and 4 really make any sense, so let's make another run at accumulating a million bucks, extending the time over which you will allow yourself to do it. This time, let's give you until age 68 to make the magic goal. Fine, then 68 − 28 = 40. Now look at the last row in Table 4. (This probably means that wealth goals for most of us that extend beyond forty years aren't worth worrying about, or we will be so old by then that we won't have a clue as to what to do with a million anyhow.)

Once again, look at Table 4 on the forty-year row, still under the 8 percent column, where you see the value 279.781. That's what $1.00 per year at an 8 percent yield will be worth in forty years, so our calculation now becomes:

$$\frac{\$1{,}000{,}000}{279.781} = \$3574.22$$

Nothing to it, you say, I can easily save that much to invest. I'm glad you're happy, but remember please that what you did was not magic. You just waited longer to satisfy your $1 million goal. There is still no tooth fairy, even after you get your six-year molars.

Let's take one last shot at figuring what it takes to get where you want to be, using our tables. This time, you set a series of intermediate wealth creation goals; you're still twenty-eight years old, but you are willing to take more risk while you're younger (to get a higher yield) and accumulate more wealth. Now you tell me that these are your new wealth creation goals:

By the time you are	you want to accumulate	and you are willing to take enough risk to earn a yield of
38	$150,000	12%
48	500,000	10%
58	1,200,000	8%
68	2,250,000	6%

It's easy to see that you are getting more cautious as you age. (Remember what we said in Chapter 2 about risk preferences changing over a lifetime.) For many, this is quite common, but your psychology aside, how can we figure out what annual investment it will take to reach all four of these goals?

First, your 38-year-old goal of $150,000. Since you're 28 now, it's the ten-year row in Table 4 that interests you. And only the 12 percent column makes sense. There, the number is 19.6546. So, the annual investment you have to make for the first ten years to reach this goal is found by:

$$\frac{\$150{,}000}{19.6546} = \$7{,}631.80$$

Now that's a steep amount to put away annually, especially at your age, but whether you have the fortitude to do it is your business and has nothing whatsoever to do with the mathematics.

Now for your goal at age 48: $500,000. You'll already have the $150,000 you've accumulated to this point working for you for the next ten years at 10 percent. To see what this grows to, go back to Table 3 and look in the ten-year row under the 10 percent column, where you better find 2.5937. This means that your $150,000 will be worth $150,000 × 2.5937 = $389,055 by age 48. And *that* means that you will only have to accumulate another $500,000 − $389,055 = 110,945 over the next ten years. You should know the drill by now! Back into Table 4, out the ten-year row, under the 10 percent column, where you see 17.5312. To figure how much you'll need to invest annually, we calculate:

$$\frac{\$110{,}945}{17.5312} = \$6{,}328.43$$

Not a pittance, by any means, but certainly no larger an annual contribution than you made during the first ten years, even at a decreased yield. And that's because the first $150,000 that you accumulated has been working for you too! Something about money begets money.

Now for your 58-year-old goal. The $500,000 you already have accumulated by age 48 will be invested at 8 percent for ten more years. From Table 3, we can see that this will amount to $500,000 × 2.1589 = $1,079,450. This leaves only $1,200,000 −

$1,079,450 = $120,550 more to be accumulated to reach your goal. Going to Table 4 in the ten-year row, under the 8 percent column, we see the value 15.6455. The amount you must contribute annually is found by:

$$\frac{\$120,550}{15.6455} = \$7,705.09$$

And finally, for your 68-year-old goal, $2,250,000. First, we'll let your $1,200,000 compound annually at 6 percent for ten years, which from Table 3 we can calculate by $1,200,000 × 1.7908 = $2,148,960. So that leaves you just $2,250,000 − $2,148,960 = $101,040 more to accumulate over the next ten years. At 6 percent now, the right value from Table 4 is 13.9716, which works out to an annual contribution of:

$$\frac{\$101,040}{13.9716} = \$7,231.81$$

So there you are. Without a PC, without fancy formulas, you can sit down with these two tables and your pencil and hand calculator, and in a couple of minutes test the reasonableness of *any* wealth creation goal that you may set for yourself. True, my tables cannot tell us whether you're being honest with yourself about risk, whether the investment you are contemplating will turn out the way you predict it will, or even whether you will be happy with your goal when you get there. But using this simple process *can* tell you quickly whether you are off on a wild goose chase or whether you're seeking a goal that makes sense for *your* financial circumstances.

So don't tell me that you aren't a quant jock, that you never were good at numbers, that you don't have a PC, and that you can't even program your hand-held calculator. No excuses! With two tables and a bit of multiplication and long division, you can be the master of your own wealth creation plan. It's as simple as that!

SHORTCUT FOR FIGURING HOW FAST YOUR MONEY DOUBLES

One time when I was a kid, a seventh-grade teacher taught me a fancy quick process for squaring any two-digit number. I have used that process for forty-five years. My dad could add up a column of ten 7-digit numbers in less than a minute and never miss. He showed me how he did it many times when I was younger, but I was never able to master it. I finally figured out my dad was smarter than me by several orders of magnitude and gave up. Since that time, I've always been interested in mathematical shortcuts—especially the practical kinds.

Burton Malkiel, economist, business school dean, and well-known author (*A Random Walk Down Wall Street,* 3rd edition, Norton, 1985) has a neat little shortcut to estimate fairly accurately when your money will double at any interest rate. It's called the rule of 72, although I cannot swear that he gave it that name. To figure out how long it takes to double your money at any interest rate compounded annually, just divide 72 by the interest rate and you have the answer. For your easy reference, here is another of my vexing tables—Table 5.

Table 5

If the interest rate is (%)	It takes about this long		for money to double (in years)
6	72/6	=	12
7	72/7	=	10.3
8	72/8	=	9
10	72/10	=	7.2
12	72/12	=	6
15	72/15	=	4.8

If you want to check Dr. Malkiel, go back to Tables 3 and 4 and work out a sample problem (to three decimal places). Unless you're a bona-fide quant jock, just accept this as an article of faith and go on to the next section. Malkiel wouldn't lie to you, and you know I won't!

WEALTH IS FOR SPENDING TOO

All of our words in this chapter on quant jocking have been about *accumulating* wealth, none about spending it. And that's a rather warped model for living. For those of you who plan to accumulate wealth until you reach your goal and then systematically spend it until there is not one penny left above what it will cost to bury you when you go, Table 6 is a handy device for implementing your scheme. (Your children will not understand either your strategy or Table 6, but it's your money so it really doesn't matter.)

Table 6

		If the balance of your wealth is earning this percent					
		5%	6%	7%	8%	9%	10%
If you withdraw this percent of your wealth each year and systematically throw it away	5%						your wealth will last you these many years
	6%	36					
	7%	25	33				
	8%	20	23	30			
	9%	16	18	22	28		
	10%	14	15	17	20	26	

An example may help. If you are sixty-five and think you will live another twenty years, you can very safely spend up to 8 percent of your accumulated wealth if it's earning 5 percent annually before it completely disappears. After twenty years, you would be 85 and broke—but very happy. If you are twenty years old and your wealth is earning 5 percent and you dissipate it double time at the rate of 10% / year, you will be thirty-four (20 + 14) when you are broke. Unless you are rich, try another row. (You know, rows go from left to right.)

And if you're still with me, let's try another chapter.

An Income-Tax Primer

The taxpayer, that's someone who works for the federal government but doesn't have to take a civil service exam.
RONALD REAGAN

REFLECTIONS

If I had written this book before February 25, 1913, I could have skipped this chapter (you could have, too). Before 1913, there was *no* federal income tax! No checks mailed to the I.R.S. center nearest you, no Form 1040s, no tax audits, and best of all no cheating and lying about income and expenses. Those were the days!

The Sixteenth Amendment to the Constitution of the United States, adopted on that infamous date, said (in part): "The Congress shall have the power to lay and collect taxes on income from whatever source derived without apportionment among the several states and without regard to any census or enumeration." Later that year, Congress passed the first law that implemented this tax on individuals. Since that date, 198,435 lawyers and 213,389 CPAs have had their hands in our pockets interpreting just what Congress had in mind! So much for representative democracy and entrepreneurship.

And it didn't stop in 1913. A good part of the time our congressional representatives and senators have spent in Washington since 1913 has been devoted to amending the tax laws, moving the "tax bite" around—from single taxpayers to married ones, from investors to salaried people and partially back to investors, from individuals to corporations and back again, and 10,000 other changes that have been made in the tax laws since their inception. This all adds up to a whole lot of effort to make sure that each citizen among us pays a "fair" share of what it costs to run the country (hardly anyone thinks his or her share is fair), and that figure is somewhere near $2 trillion now. In numerical form, that's $2,000,000,000,000 (twelve zeros, count 'em). Makes the check you sent with your form 1040 last year (or the one you got back) seem kind of insignificant, doesn't it?

Paying taxes is like disposing of nuclear waste: Everyone recognizes the need for it, but no one wants it in *their* backyard. In the last twenty-five years, I cannot recall meeting anyone who fulfilled either their ego needs or their need to achieve by paying taxes—even their fair share. But successful wealth creation absolutely, undeniably, unequivocably, and permanently requires you to be familiar with the basic ideas of income taxation—not to the point that you program your phone with the number of a tax partner in a law firm, but at least to the point that you *understand* the effect of income taxes on your income and your wealth.

THE HIT

If you're single and your gross adjusted income is less than $17,850 a year, the feds want 15 percent of it. (If so, you probably checked this book out of the library, instead of buying it.) If you and your spouse file jointly and your "gross adjusted income" (a term that has made billions for CPAs, including mine) is between $29,750 and $71,900, then the feds want 28 percent of it. And if it's higher than $71,900, they want even more, 33 percent. (Keep in mind that Congress rewrites the tax code faster than dress designers change hemlines. The figures here are *this* year's fashion; see pages 240–42 for all incomes and tax rates.)

And it doesn't stop there. Besides federal and state income taxes, there is social security tax and in some areas, such as New York City, city income tax as well. We won't dwell on social security simply because no one has yet come up with a way to avoid it, which is certainly not true of federal, state, and city income taxes. Suffice it to say, before you turn around, you can and will be systematically relieved of about 28 percent of your income by the feds alone if you are in the middle of our $20,000–$70,000 annual income range. And if you are very successful and keep getting raises until you earn above $71,900, those kindly federal tax folks will wind up with about 33 percent of it! A much shorter way to say all this would be to note that most income taxes are progressive: As you make more money, you have to pay a higher and higher percentage of it in taxes. If you are serious about creating wealth, you need to keep an eagle eye on the income tax you pay *and* all of the legal ways you can reduce it. Nothing less will do!

A SHORT HANDFUL OF DEFINITIONS

Tax folk have a language all their own—that's what lets them charge people up to $250 an hour to talk with them. Since it took most of them five to seven years to learn this language, you and I can't do it in part of a chapter, but what we can (and will) do is learn something about four tax terms that have a lot to do with wealth creation (and retention too):

- Tax deductions
- Tax deferrals
- Tax shelters
- Tax-free income

So let's discuss each of these terms in turn, not to master tax law but to make us conversant with those who *do* master the law.

TAX DEDUCTIONS

These are any legal subtractions for you to use to reduce your taxable income. The government(s) lets you deduct items from your income to make it a smaller number, so that when you multiply your taxable income by the tax rate, the tax you owe is smaller too. The list of deductions is nearly (but not quite) endless; a longer (but still not quite endless) list can be found in the Form 1040 instructions that you get absolutely free about February of every year. Anyhow, here goes:

- Other taxes (state tax, property tax, sales tax)
- Medical and dental expenses (above a certain percentage)

- Interest you pay on *some* debts (mortgages qualify, some consumer loans don't)
- Contributions you make to qualified charities (this generally does not include your spouse or brother, but can include your children if your tax adviser is smart enough)
- Losses you suffer (roof falls in, house burns up without insurance)
- What you pay your tax adviser to be creative for you
- Money you spend to support certain others (parents, for instance)
- 13,429 other things including: uniforms, subscriptions to journals that are supposed to help you learn (including how to pay less tax), professional dues, and college professors' writing expenses
- What you paid for this book!

The key word here is *deductibility*—whether the I.R.S. will let you *deduct* any or all of these expenditures from your income. And that is exactly what a good tax adviser will help you decide. (Whether you need a tax adviser and how to pick one and learn to love him or her is one of the things we'll talk about in some detail in Chapter 7. Right now, we're defining.)

So what's it all mean? If you (and/or your tax adviser) come up with an extra $1,000 of deductions next year, and your tax bracket (federal and state combined) is, say, 35%, then you save $1,000 × 35% = $350 in taxes next April. If you are frugal and put that in an 8 percent investment and leave it and its yearly interest compounding there for twenty years, Table 3 from Chapter 4 will tell you that you'll have earned $350 × 4.661 = $1631.35. If you (and your tax adviser) are as smart next year (and each year thereafter) and find another $1,000 of deductibles (and that's not nearly as hard as you think), and if you keep putting the $350 this saves you into your annually compounding 8 percent investment, then Table 4 from Chapter 4 shows you that you will have $350 × 49.4229 = $17,298.02 in twenty years. And *that's* what a single $1,000 annual deduction can do for you! (With discipline, of course.)

TAX DEFERRALS

A famous senator from Mississippi, who was at one time chairman of the Senate Finance Committee, said, "There's nothing that says a man has to take a toll bridge across a river when there is a free bridge nearby." I wonder what happened to people in Washington who thought like that. *Deferring* taxes is not the same as having them permanently forgiven by the I.R.S. It's more like "due now, but pay later." We know you owe us the money, Gloria, but if you jump through these three or four technical hoops, you can pay us the tax five years from today—even thirty-five years from today, in some cases. Oh, you say, that's very nice of you, I.R.S., but my parents always taught me never to put off until tomorrow what should be done today. Only in the real world, Gloria! In the arcane world of income taxes, always, always, always (cross your heart and promise me you will never forget this) defer taxes when it's legal!

How *do* you get taxes deferred? There are many ways (including some excellent ones discussed in detail in Chapter 8), but for now consider my personal situation. Under Federal Statute 403-B, I am permitted to defer up to $9,500 of my annual earnings until I retire. This means that if I elect to do it (you guess whether or not I do), I don't pay taxes on that until I retire and begin spending it. That's a deferral, and a good one, reserved unfortunately for educators and employees of tax-exempt organizations. (Would you consider changing your employer?) There are many opportunities to *defer* current income taxes available to a wide variety of salaried people, but more on that in Chapter 8.

What does a deferral mean to *your* bottom line? Suppose you are allowed to defer the taxes on 10 percent of your current income until you retire (say in thirty years), and further suppose that your current income is $40,000 a year . . . let's leave it at $40,000 with no increases for thirty years, but only to make the arithmetic simpler. Ten percent of your salary is $4,000, and say your federal and state taxes combined are 30 percent. What happens is that for thirty years, you don't pay $4,000 × 30% = $1,200 income taxes. The law lets you invest that $4,000 each year (but not spend it, mind you), so let's do it for thirty years at, say, an 8 percent yield. Table 4 tells us that the wealth you will have created at that time is $4,000 × 122.3459 = $489,384 (and we haven't paid a cent of tax on it or on the interest either). That's a deferral. Of course, doomsday is coming and you will owe tax on it, but not for thirty years! And, who knows, taxes may be abolished by then.

Remember, please, you *still* have to live, buy beer, raise your children, make car payments, and pay off loans, so you may *not* be able to afford to invest $4,000 a year, but may need to *spend* part of it to live! In that case, your deferral is less but still very worthwhile, so defer all that you can. Deferral is the best deal going.

There are at least four good reasons why you should defer paying as much tax as you can possibly manage:

- *The time value of money:* We've just seen with a couple of examples that money mounts up because of compound interest.
- *Inflation:* There is always *some* inflation in our economy, and whatever taxes you defer you will pay in later years with money worth *less*—that is, with *cheaper dollars.* Here's a way to make inflation work for you!
- *Forced savings:* Just like the RIF (reduction in force) I told you about in Chapter 3, deferring taxes is forced savings. If

you can train yourself to drink cheaper beer, you wind up with a bigger wad in the future.

- *Possibility of lower tax rates in the future:* If you look back twenty years, tax rates have trended downward during that time; if you understand politics, you know that raising taxes is the stuff that recall elections are made of. So go with the possibilities that tax rates will continue to fall; if time proves you wrong, you will still have all that accumulated compound interest (tax free all during the time it has piled up) to bail yourself out!

TAX SHELTERS

Although the 1986 tax bill put a fair-sized dent in these, the animal is still alive and kicking for many of us. A tax shelter is an investment that, at least for a period of time, produces losses that you then use to "offset" other taxable income you've earned. That's a lot in one sentence, so let's look at an example. Suppose you buy a house across town as an investment and rent it to someone. As expenses, you can charge repairs, property taxes, utilities (if you pay them), the interest you pay on the mortgage (if there is one), and an annual charge for depreciation (which is theoretically the "wearing out" of the house). In the early years at least, when interest on the mortgage is at its highest and when you are deducting depreciation (we'll talk in detail about this entire process in Chapter 11), the house will actually show a loss—that is, the expenses we just listed will be more than the rental income you get. This loss is a "shelter" in that you can use it to offset some other taxable income you earn. Say, for instance, you have a taxable income (from your salary) of $40,000 and your rental house "loses" $5,000. In this instance, you would pay taxes on only $35,000 ($40,000 − $5,000). The loss on your rental house "shelters" $5,000 of taxable income. Shelters it from what, you ask? The Internal Revenue Service.

But why would I buy a house to rent if it loses money, you ask? Excellent question. The answer is that there are losses and there are losses. For example, your house produces a tax-deductible loss (total rental income less total expenses) but doesn't actually lose real cash money because of depreciation. Depreciation is a noncash expense—that is, you never write anybody a check for the depreciation. It's strictly an accounting entry, an allowance for wearing out. It's a terrific way to dodge the I.R.S. and it's legal too!

Of course, someday when you sell the house for more than your accountant says it's worth, you'll have to pay taxes on the profit you made (buy low, sell high), but that may be twenty years from now and in the meantime you can accumulate the taxes you save and invest them at compound interest—you know the routine from here, by now! It turns out that "postponing doomsday" like this is the foundation of tax shelters. Don't fret. We'll have a great deal more to say about all of this in Chapter 11.

TAX-FREE INCOME

Is there really such a thing? You bet there is. The interest on many bonds that cities and counties (municipalities) issue to raise money to do nice things such as build parks, schools, jails, and roads is *free* of federal taxes and usually from state taxes if you file in the state that issues the bond. Now if that sounds like a permanent bonanza, think again and remember, there's no free lunch. The municipalities that sell these bonds know the holders don't pay tax on the interest, so they lower the interest rate to reflect that fact. After all, if you were given a choice of a 10 percent yield fully taxable at say 40 percent (this would cost you 4 percent for income taxes, leaving you a 6 percent return) or a 7 of your 10 percent municipal yield, absolutely free of taxes, you'd be foolish not to go for the 7 percent deal. After all, it's a whole percentage point higher yield, and that mounts up fast. Generally, for people in higher tax brackets, these "tax-frees" make sense, and we'll have a lot more to say about how much sense they make in Chapter 10.

Before we leave tax-free income, we need to cover one small piece of arithmetic. In my example above of comparing a fully-taxable and a tax-free yield, the answer was too obvious—7 percent is always better than 6 percent (if the risk is the same). Often, however, comparisons of taxable versus tax-free yields aren't that easy, and a bit of algebraic skulduggery will be a big help in these situations. To find the taxable equivalent yield to any tax-free yield, you do this:

$$\text{Taxable equivalent yield} = \frac{\text{Tax-free yield}}{1 - \text{your tax rate}}$$

Your tax rate is 35 percent and a tax-free municipal bond is paying a 6 percent yield. What would you have to get as a yield on a fully taxable investment to equal this?

$$\begin{aligned}\text{Answer} &= \frac{0.06}{1 - 0.35} \\ &= \frac{0.06}{0.65} \\ &= 9.23\%\end{aligned}$$

If anybody comes along and offers you a taxable investment with a yield less than 9.23 percent and claims it's as good as your 6 percent tax-free yield, offer them an option on the Brooklyn Bridge real cheap.

SUMMARY

A *deduction* is anything you subtract from taxable income to reduce your tax bite. A *deferral* is income on which any taxes due will be payable later rather than now. A *shelter* is an investment that produces losses for a while that can be subtracted from your other income to reduce your final tax bill. And *tax-free income* is just that: income on which there is no tax, period.

TIME FOR A SHORT QUIZ

A friend stops you on the street and says he just bought the rights to scrape barnacles off the underside of the Lincoln Tunnel for $500,000. Why, that's insane you reply. Barnacles are bringing only 10 cents a pound and the cost of scraping them and bringing them up is well over a dollar a pound. I know, your friend says, but I did it for a tax-write off. Question: How would you evaluate your friend's knowledge of taxes? Answer: He doesn't know beans about taxes! If he gets involved in scraping barnacles, he'll lose 90¢ for every pound, and if he gets his volume up he'll really lose lots of money in addition to the $500,000 he's already paid for this dubious deal. Of course, if he insists to the I.R.S. that barnacle-scraping is a legitimate business and that someday he'll make a go of it, they'll let him deduct the 90¢ loss on every pound from his otherwise taxable income. But if his tax rate is, say, 40%, then every 90¢ he loses in the barnacle business was really worth only 90¢ × 40% = 36¢ to him in taxes reduced on his other income. In short, your friend loses 90¢ − 36¢ = 54¢ real money on every pound in this dumb scheme (plus the half million)—and that's *after* he has deducted the value to him of the tax loss on the barnacle business. Moral: There are tax shelters and tax shelters. You want the ones that make sense—the good deals on their own merits that also carry some tax benefits. Losing real money isn't fun, and you shouldn't do it!

BEING LEGAL VERSUS BEING STUPID

Sooner or later, every one of us is confronted with a chance to cheat on our taxes. It happens in overt ways—someone pays you in cash for a service you performed—or in subtle ways—you've been sending your mother $50 a month and at tax time you sit there reflecting whether it would be okay to claim her as a dependent. If you do either, you are cheating; sorry, but it's as simple as that. So what *do* you do?

I had a friend, let's call him Sam, who owned a thriving business. Once a week, he sent his truck north with a load of product. Sam was very bright, and he noticed that the truck returned empty. Sam made a deal for the truck to carry cargo back, but it was an "off the books" deal. Sam was (just as we all have been tempted to do) cheating on his taxes. Sam made money (lots of it, since he didn't have to pay any taxes) hauling cargo back. Only three people knew about the "deal": Sam, the truck driver, and the person who kept the books. One day, the truck driver got mad at Sam over something and threatened to turn him in. Sam called the driver's bluff. When Sam came to trial, the bookkeeper testified for the government to get immunity. When all the testimony was over and the judge had to rule (always ask for a non-jury trial if you've been going around screwing other people), he looked down from the bench at my friend Sam and started his sentence with words I shall remember the rest of my life: "When I was a kid, my father made me work and save money . . . " Oh Lord, I thought, here it comes.

Sam spent eleven months in a federal prison—but at one of those military bases where you can play golf, read, and reflect on how stupid you were. Sam's golf and tennis games improved, he acquired a terrific suntan, and he still reflects on how stupid he was. You can't win! At least not when three people know!

THREE REASONS YOU SHOULD PLAY THE TAX GAME STRAIGHT

- You are too smart not to.
- There are entirely too many legal ways to beat the I.R.S.
- The yield on tax-cheating is low—drugs, starting a new religion, and bank robbing all return more!

So don't cheat. And now let's visit my friends the bankers!

6

Banks Can Be Bad for Your Wealth

A bank is a place where they lend you an umbrella in fair weather and ask for it back when it begins to rain. ROBERT FROST

Do banks give you a warm, safe feeling? I don't mean the suburban branch banks, like islands in the parking lots of shopping malls. I mean the downtown banks, the temples to money with doric columns and marble floors, a vault with safe deposit boxes, and a lot of tasteful art. Safety. Solidity. Here for the ages. Architecture and decor sending us the message: This is an *institution!* Trust us. We will take *care* of your money. (But not of you.) Oops! Did I really write that? Well, friends, it's true. That "institution" downtown is a profit center too, and most of the wealth that banks create is on behalf of their shareholders—not you. Yes, most banks are safe and solid, and they *charge* you for safety. (Did you ever think of shopping around to see who charges less?) This chapter suggests what you should allow banks to do with your money and how you should deal with bankers—to the benefit of *your* wealth creation strategy.

WHY USE A BANK?

Simple—mattresses burn up, and when they do, it's nearly impossible to persuade your insurance agent that you had $50,000 under it in small bills. Bank checking accounts and passbook savings accounts are a great place for a little bit of money, but they are the worst possible place to park a *lot* of money. Banks offer better deals than these, which we'll cover in Chapter 9. Banks are not unsafe—heavens, no, your money is legally safe up to $100,000 per depositor, and historically the Federal Reserve System (the daddy of all banks, run out of Washington) has made good on nearly all bank deposits when banks have failed. No, checking and savings accounts are bad places to stash more money than you need for *transactions* needs (remember that word from Chapter 3) because *they pay such low rates of interest compared to other equally safe investments.*

However, each of us needs one or two banks (why more than one is explained later in this chapter) as a *temporary* repository for our money, a place we can safely inventory enough money to get us through this month (and maybe the next two or three, too). A bank is a reasonable place to keep money for short periods of time because it affords us maximum liquidity (you'll remember that term, too, from Chapter 3). We can get our hands on the money whenever the bank is open (usually nine to five weekdays) and up to several hundred dollars even when it's shut by using the bank's ATM (automatic teller machine). This saves getting our cousin Charlie to cash a check for us, or bothering the folks down at the gas station.

But—please note this—banks are a bad place to:

- Keep a lot of money in checking and savings (they make more on it than you do)
- Get financial advice on how to create wealth (most bankers know very little about this)
- Leave a business in your will for them to run (they know even less about how to do this successfully)
- Spend time on a rainy day (the only chairs are next to desks of folks who want to make you a car loan—go to a movie instead!)

In fairness to our banking friends, we need to point out that banks offer investments that *do* pay higher rates of interest than checking and savings accounts. What these are and how to take advantage of them will be discussed in Chapter 9.

WOULD YOU LET YOUR DAUGHTER MARRY ONE?

About a fifth of the men and women in MBA programs go into commercial banking. They are nice young people, they dress well, they wind up in the upper half of their class academically, they are a bit better looking than the average student, they are honest, and they are respectful to their professors. They do not like to take risk, they prefer to work in surroundings that provide staff support for problems that arise, their lifetime earnings come out much less than the average MBA student, and they exhibit lower aggressiveness, independence, and entrepreneurial skills than most other students. Most of them enter banking for what the architecture and decor promise: safety, security, a planned and structured environment, an institution. They're there to avoid taking major risks—not for the money!

You will have to deal with bankers, and, like parking-lot attendants, if you know what makes them tick, your chances of getting your car back without damage increases. The same with your money! So a bit of time spent right now looking at who they are, how they think, and what turns them on and off will be time well spent for you as you pursue *your* wealth goal. (And always remember, it's *your* goal, not theirs.)

THE ROAD TO THE TOP

In every profession, there are things you need to do and things you need to avoid if you are interested in "moving up." Banking is no exception. Bankers, from day one, are trained in orderliness—to make sure every *i* is dotted and every *t* is crossed in dealing with money. That's a great characteristic if they are to look after my $746 and not lose a cent. When they lend me money, it's the same routine, only more so: every *i* dotted, every *t* crossed, and every word triple checked. They are trained (from the beginning) to get everything down in writing (all signed by you and your spouse) so that the bank can't lose. That's right—*can't lose*. In point of fact, banks take very little real risk, and when it comes to lending you (the typical salaried person) money, they take nearly zero risk.

A successful banking career *can* be ruined by bad loans. Not one bad car loan he makes to you (they can always come and get what's left of the car) and not one bad $1,000 personal loan she might make to you (they can seize your checking and savings accounts so fast you won't know where they went if you fail to repay). But a series of loans that go bad, cause problems, require consequential collection effort, or in any way get the attention of their boss can show a banker the slow lane if not the back door. The career payoff is clearly on the side of excessive prudence, safety, and conservatism, and that means tying you up nice and tight. Polite, yes, but always nice and tight!

COLUMNS AND ROWS

Bankers like orderliness, as I said. When you go in to get money, it's always better for you to have a nice answer for (1) why you need it, and (2) how you intend to pay it back. They love written plans with orderly columns of figures. A faculty friend of mine went into one of our local banks and asked to borrow $75,000 to start a bicycle shop. After suggesting that any university faculty member who wanted to open a bike shop had to be suffering from temporary insanity, the banker asked my friend for his financial plan—his "proformas" as they call them (financial plans, all done up in nice neat columns and rows showing where every penny will come from and where it will eventually go). My friend was dumbstruck. He wouldn't have known a proforma if you had run him over with one. He left the bank disillusioned about the free enterprise system and thoroughly confused. Later that day, he dropped by my office and asked me what a proforma was. And, voila, in less than thirty minutes, using my PC, he and I built a beautiful one. It had projected profit and loss statements, gorgeous balance sheets, all kinds of cash flow projections, and all the bells and whistles that turn on a banker. I asked him to (1) get a nice-looking plastic binder to contain all this paperwork, and (2) wait a couple of weeks before he went back to the banker (so the banker wouldn't figure out what he had done). He walked in two weeks later, threw his "financial plan" on the desk, and had the $75,000 in two days. He went into business and was bankrupt in less than a year. So much for what turns bankers on—columns and rows, neatly done—not bicycles or business. Get it?

YOU'VE GOTTA HAVE HEART

Perhaps you think I ought to cut bankers a little slack—I've been rough on them here. After all, they're nice folks, trying to do their job, get ahead, and even create some wealth on *their* salary, but they work under a *very rigid* system that leaves precious little room for innovation, discretion, and *heart*. Bankers work in a system where their decision-making authority is severely limited, where the authority of each person to make lending decisions is tightly defined, and where infractions or indiscretions are easily disclosed and quickly punished. This leaves them with considerably less authority than they may represent to you, and a very restricted ability to use "heart" in lending or collecting. Heart they may have, but heart they ain't paid to use on the job!

When you apply for a home loan, a school loan, a car loan, or any other kind of loan for that matter, and your banker (even a vice president) says to you "There are a couple of details I need to work on before *I* can say yes or no" or "I have a very important meeting this afternoon, so would it be okay if I called you tomorrow," you can read that as: "My boss is in Richmond and won't be back until tomorrow morning, and he has to sign off on your application, so I'll have to put you off without me looking bad and here's the line I'll use." He's warm, he's sincere, but he's not exactly loaded with authority.

Every banking officer knows his lending limits (the amount of money and loan terms). And, more to the point, regardless of how much he likes you, how much heart he really has, and how much he wants to help you, rules are rules (if you want to get ahead). You just can't have thousands of folks running around the bank lending money to other folks who might never pay it back, right? Right, and judicious application of this principle got U.S. banks on the string for $100 billion of Latin American debt, the value of which is now much less than $100 billion!

THE FIRST RULE

The cardinal rule for you to remember in banking is that *everything* is negotiable. That's right, everything! That doesn't mean that your buddy in Branch #436 can make you a car loan for sixty months if four years is the bank's limit, but it *does* mean that somebody in that bank *can* (and will do so if he or she believes that doing so best serves the *bank's* interests). Yes, everything *is* negotiable in a bank. What is involved is finding *who* has the authority and figuring out a way to deal with *that* person. You get to that person through your buddy, around your buddy, with your buddy, or over your buddy, but if you want an exception, you need to find out who can grant it. Make no mistake, friends, I am not saying to you that the president of Citicorp will give you ten more days to make your car payment when it's already three months overdue. If that's your situation, you screwed up and now you have to bear it. What I *am* saying is that if you need a car loan with unusual terms (terms that are not in the bank's consumer lending manual), if you are a good customer, and if you press hard enough, chances are good *someone* will work it out for you! That's what negotiable means. All you have to do is find the right person.

One more point and I'll quit. It's *always* easier (and better) to find the person in the bank hierarchy who has the authority to do what you need. So don't sit there and call your buddy who is helping you a low-paid, authority-bereft, risk-avoiding twit. Go ahead and co-opt him to help you find the person who can make it happen. And when he does, make sure your friend gets *all* the credit.

WHEN TO BORROW AND WHEN NOT TO BORROW

It's a fact: If you don't borrow, you will be old by the time you save enough money to buy something big. A dress, a suit, a trip to New York, or a set of Macgregor clubs, these things you generally can buy out of current income or savings. But a car, a house, or a three-month trip to Africa—these things are better financed by borrowing. The number of things it's possible to put into both lists (the borrow-for and don't borrow-for lists) are endless, so let's do it the generic way, with some rules for when to borrow and when not to. Its's okay to borrow money:

- When the situation is absolutely life-threatening (sickness, imminent repossession of your house or car, or missed child-support payments)
- When you want to establish credit (that's right, the best way to do this is to borrow when you *don't* need the money so that later you can borrow when you do—it's weird, but remember what I told you about bankers; and besides, it'll only cost you a few bucks in interest to establish that you are creditworthy, so later you can borrow when you are not creditworthy, got it?)
- When you want to buy something big (that you *can* afford) but don't have the cash for at present (like a car—drive now, pay later)
- When you can earn more than it costs you to borrow, considering taxes, of course (if a bank will loan you money for 6 percent and you can get 9 percent in tax-free bond interest, do it!)
- When you intend to use the money to purchase a tax-deferred investment (if you can borrow for 8 percent and buy a tax-deferred, fairly risk-free deal that pays 8 percent, you still may be better off to borrow and buy it to avoid the tax and the tax on the interest every year; if you are thoroughly confused now, reread parts of Chapters 4 and 5, and pay special attention to Chapter 10 when you get there)
- When you are "between deals" and need cash (say you have a house worth $90,000 and you are moving to a new city where you see a house you love for $90,000, it's okay to borrow the downpayment on the new house until you sell the old one); however, remember to watch what the payments on the loan will be and decide whether you can manage it
- When you can borrow for substantially less than what you are paying on your credit card accounts (say you owe an

outstanding balance on your cards with interest at 18% and you can borrow somewhere else at 10%—do it now.)

You should *avoid* the temptation to borrow money:

- When you believe you have already borrowed up to a prudent limit—that is, when it will be difficult if not impossible for you to pay your loans back under the terms of your loan agreements (all you do here is permanently damage your credit)
- When you are going to use the loan proceeds to buy something you would like to have but really can't afford (at least not this year—be honest!)
- When you are going to use the proceeds to buy investments that are entirely too risky for you (if you are waffling here, reread parts of Chapter 2 on risk)
- When the lender (bank, insurance company, small loan company, etc.) is pressuring you into loan terms you don't like and you have some time to reconsider (negotiating is all over once you sign the note)

IF YOU'VE NEVER HAD ANY, HOW DO YOU GET SOME?

It's difficult to believe that anyone in America over the age of eight has never borrowed money, but it's true. Many don't believe in it, some classify credit cards as instruments of the devil, and others believe that owing money makes you eligible to be drafted earlier in time of war. But the question remains, if you've never used credit, how do you establish it in the first place? Answer: If you are a woman who has used her husband's credit for years, it's difficult. If you are a young person applying for a credit card for the first time, it's still difficult. If you are black, female, under twenty-five, and have just taken your first full-time job, it's all the more difficult. (We'll have more to say in a minute or two about discrimination in lending against women, but for now it's getting credit that counts.) What you must do is:

- Open a checking account and a small savings account at a *local* bank (preferably the newest bank in town); don't overdraw either, please!
- Fill out the forms a lender will require (a statement of what you own and what it's worth; a statement of what you earn and from whom; and some other intimate information, mostly legal these days)
- Apply for charge accounts from two or three local stores; charge a few things you can afford to buy and *pay the account on time*
- Apply for credit cards (Master Charge and/or Visa) *through the bank in which you have accounts*
- Don't get discouraged (remember I told you that bankers and other credit-granting folks are genetically risk averse)

Above all, don't quit! If you try all these things and nothing good happens, get your Mom, Dad, sister, or main squeeze to sign with you—that is, to guarantee to pay your debts if you can't. Before you do this, make the lender state *when* she will permit you to set up your *own* credit accounts if you have a cosigner to begin with.

Credit is a two-way street: What you borrow, you have to pay back—and on time too! The better you do this, the more they will lend you. By the time you have been in the credit business for five years, you should be able to borrow at least 10 percent of your annual salary on *your signature*—that is, without pledging specific assets (such as your car) for collateral. At that time, your credit-card limits (Visa or Mastercard) should be the same—10 percent of your salary—but be careful, these cards charge interest (if you don't pay them off promptly each month) at somewhere between 12 and 18 percent, which is murderous! Credit-card interest rates can be one and a half to two times the prime rate (what banks say they charge their best corporate *and individual* customers), so be careful about letting credit-card balances mount up without paying them promptly!

One final note about "earning" a line of credit. If you do what we suggest, and over time your bank gets to know you and decides that you are "creditworthy" (at least up to a limit), you

should make arrangements so that you can "trigger" that line of credit by phone—that is, call your banker and say you want $5,000 deposited in your checking account *now*. If you are in Seattle on a vacation and run into a great buy in art, there are only two or three ways to pay for it: (1) write the artist a check (if you have the money, this is great; if not, it is illegal); (2) use your credit card (if your limit is that high); or (3) use an expensive overdraft (what banks call "easy credit" or "instant credit," usually hooked to your checking account). This latter arrangement usually carries an interest rate comparable to a credit card—in any event, *much* higher than a "signature" loan (the one you just sign for and get the money without pledging anything). Being able to call your banker and get money put in your account on a line of credit (at normal interest rates) is a good goal for you to work toward!

BE CAREFUL WHAT YOU SIGN

Your signature is a potent weapon. It will open doors, get you a marriage license, or bind you to a three-year baseball contract. And for $10, you can have it analyzed. If you put it on a financial obligation, however (a note, mortgage, and stuff like that), it is for real—as in *permanent*—and folks will hound you forever until you pay.

Always read *every word* of what you sign, especially when someone is in a hurry for you to sign it. Read it until you understand it. Ask questions; don't be embarrassed. Although you may sign a thousand financial documents in your lifetime, the list of don'ts is fairly short. Here it is:

- Don't sign anything that lets the lender come after *you* if you can't make the payments on time (let them take the car, even the house if you have to, but let that be the limit); in lending this is called "no recourse"—i.e., they can't come and make off with your first-born child if you default!
- Don't give the lender any claim on "incidental collateral"—that's their fancy name for things of value put up to secure the loan *beyond* the thing you are borrowing on (if you are borrowing against your house, let the house be the collateral and don't give them a claim on your family farm too!).
- Always keep your borrowings separate; don't let your default on one loan permit the lender to declare all your other notes due and payable right then (be sure to read the fine print to see if there is such a "tie-in" provision in what you are signing). If so, don't sign!
- If you co-sign a note for a friend (when the lender won't give your friend credit unless you do), or if you are one of several friends who are guaranteeing payment, make sure the limit of *your* liability (in dollars please) is clearly spelled out in the loan agreement. Otherwise, you may be signing away your financial life (friendship has limits too!).

Of course, all of this good advice may have to go by the boards if you are down to your last cent and they put some papers in front of you! A few years back, my wife, Charlotte, built some apartments out of her checkbook, with a promise from a mortgage banker that he would take care of us (make us a nice loan) when they were done. When her checkbook was bereft of further dollars, we called our mortgage person who informed us he was not making those kinds of loans now that money was so tight. Someone gave me the phone number of a mortgage lender who advertised that "he had money every day at a price," and I took it. After all, we were out of cash. At the closing, they presented us with a note and deed of trust to sign that was twenty-seven pages long and full of the same kinds of restrictions I just exhorted you to avoid! After two hours of my asking my lawyer, Skip, (who passed away last year) to explain all these things to us (during which time the lender's lawyer was getting both richer and angrier), I asked Skip in desperation "What do all these things mean?" "Dick," he said, "it means that if you want the money, you and Charlotte just sign right there." Skip had such away with words! If you are pressed, yield when you have to. If you don't have to, stick it to them!

LET'S HEAR IT FOR A.P.R.

Not being misled by lenders' published interest rates used to be a real hassle! Terms such as simple interest, add-on interest, daily interest, and discount interest made life miserable for borrowers who were not at ease with the complexities of interest-rate formulas. Enter Uncle Sam. As of 1968, all lenders were required to publish their A.P.R. figure for loans. A.P.R. means annual percentage rate you are paying, no ifs, ands, or buts either. When you see A.P.R., that's exactly the interest rate that converts everything to one common denominator (including "points" paid on a mortgage loan), using one set of standard interest formulas. When you are comparing interest rates charged on loans (or given on deposits too) among different financial institutions, 10.8 percent A.P.R. is better than 10.9 percent A.P.R. (This assumes that you are a borrower; if you are a depositor, 10.8 percent is worse, but you figured that out already!)

What this means for *you* is that you don't have to worry about converting published rates to a common standard; you can believe what you see written if it says "A.P.R." What this means for *lenders* is that after 1968 they had to stop misleading millions of unsuspecting folks with clever advertising about their interest rates. And what this means to *me* is that what would have been a long, tedious, boring section of the book years ago will end right here!

A.P.R. ON HOW MUCH MONEY AND UNDER WHAT CONDITIONS

The appearance of annual percentage rate interest made things simple for many who want to compare *interest rates*. But, as you know, earnings on your deposits are computed by:

Amount you have deposited	×	Interest rate they pay	×	How long you keep it deposited

This simple formula is made more complex if you consider how often a financial institution compounds the interest it pays you. Fortunately, we covered that little nuance in Chapter 4, so we can skip it here as long as you remember that the more frequent the compounding, the better off you are. What I *do* want you to remember are the two things that can increase or decrease the actual amount of interest you receive, say on your savings account:

- What penalties and service fees the financial institution charges you against your savings account.
- How the financial institution computes the amount of money in your account on which they'll pay you interest.

Fees are now a big thing with banks and other financial institutions. This makes it more difficult for you to find the true interest your savings will earn at various institutions. Some banks charge you a fee if you keep your savings account open less than a year. And some banks charge you a service charge if you let your savings account get below a certain limit—sort of like saying "Now that your account balance makes you a small fish, we'll behave as if it isn't worth our while to have you as a saver." There are cases where the service charge is more than the interest the bank pays. Fortunately, most financial institutions tell you (in advance) what this service charge is; so if they don't, ask! Although we have a truth-in-lending law in this country (the one that gave us A.P.R.), we don't yet have a "truth-in-depositing" law (this would make sense out of all the interest rates, fees, service charges, and deals that financial institutions use to confuse depositors). In Chapter 9, we'll show you how to figure out these bank deals to *your* benefit.

You would think that if you had $1,000 in your savings account there would be no question about what the bank paid you interest on! Yes, you would think that, but, Virginia, it just isn't so! There are *at least* (financial legerdemain has no bounds) a short handful of ways financial institutions count how much of your money they intend to pay interest on; here are a few words about each of them:

- *Day of deposit to day of withdrawal*: This is the *best* deal you can get—it means you earn interest on exactly, absolutely every penny you have in your account from the time you put it in there until you take it out.
- *Low balance*: This deal gives you credit for the entire interest period (a month, a quarter, a year) only for the *lowest* amount you had in your account—a real financial jerking around indeed!
- *First-in, first-out*: This scheme gives you credit for your deposits from the time you put them in until the end of the interest period, *but* charges any withdrawal you make to the balance in your account at the *beginning* of the interest period (or sometimes to the day you made your first deposit). Score: Bank: 1, Depositor, 0.
- *Last-in, first-out*: Here, the bank subtracts each withdrawal you make from your *most recent* previous deposit, and then calculates interest.

Prudent savers should *always* rank these four methods (from best to worst) like this:

- Day of deposit to day of withdrawal (best)
- Last-in, first-out
- First-in, first-out
- Low balance (worst)

One final note about savings accounts: If your savings account is inactive for a couple of years (no deposits and no withdrawals), the financial institution is allowed under the law to *assume* you have died. It then turns your money over to the state you are in under a law called "escheats." All nice and legal, and the money they turn over gets put to good use (university funding in North Carolina), but nevertheless being "escheated" out of your money is no fun, so if your account is inactive, write the bank a card once a year saying you *are* alive, and they can't touch a penny! And a penny is about what you'll have if they have been crediting interest using the low balance method and charging you service fees and penalties galore!

SWITCH GEARS TO CHECKING ACCOUNTS

As banking has become more competitive, and as banks have had to start paying interest on the money in your checking account (something they wouldn't have dreamed of doing prior to the late 1970s in competition with money market accounts), they have been forced to "make up the deficit" somewhere. And that somewhere is in fees and service charges on your checking account. After all, you didn't really think that all that interest you were getting on your checking account was gravy, did you? As a matter of fact, these fees rose more than 12 percent in one year (1985 to 1986). Charges for bounced checks rose dramatically, as did charges on small-balance checking accounts. Most banks require you to open a noninterest-bearing checking account before they will issue you a credit card. But when you finish Chapter 9, you'll be a lot more comfortable figuring all this out.

What this all means is that some research on your part is a *must* before you make any decision about opening a checking (or savings) account. To do less is to invite the financial institution to do more (and to you!). Shop for a place to keep your money the way you would shop for good clothes. Ask questions such as "Exactly what would I get from this money under these conditions?" as you'd check out the warranty for parts and labor on your new video camera and recorder. And never be timid about any of this. Financial institutions buy and sell money; that's all they do. Oddly enough, although consumers of goods such as VCRs, stereos, 35 mm cameras, and microwave ovens are extremely aware of differences in prices and features among brands, that is often not the case with people who use banks. Service charges and features can vary a lot; yet most people don't seem aware of the differences nor are they inclined to shop hard. Be a shrewd customer. You need banking services, but you don't have to stick with the same bank you've always used. Ask. And negotiate.

SOME OF OUR BEST CUSTOMERS ARE WOMEN

It's a fact that banks have discriminated against women and probably still do. A survey of 173 members of the National Association of Women Business Owners showed that over 60 percent of those who were denied commercial loans between 1980 and 1985 felt they had been discriminated against. Almost 30 percent (of those who got loans) felt the loan terms were discriminatory. And this insidious discrimination is not limited to women in business either. Just try to borrow money if you are divorced, living apart, have a joint account with your husband, or are widowed! Under the Equal Credit Opportunity Act of 1975, the same credit-granting criteria the financial institution applies to its male customers must be applied to you as a woman. They are *not* allowed to consider sex, marital status, birth control methods you may be using, or child care. Okay, so we have a law that is supposed to protect you in credit-seeking. There are still things you need to do *by* and *for* yourself that will make it easier for you to survive in a world that doesn't always heed to the spirit of this law! These include:

- Make sure the credit history of any joint accounts you have with your husband shows up in both your names (until you do this, don't let him die, please).
- Make sure your credit cards *are* your credit cards and not simply duplicates of your husband's card (just write, call, or holler, and the credit card company has to tell you this).
- Resist any attempt by a company to deny you credit when your marital status changes (agree to file another credit application if they demand it, but don't let them shut you out till they evaluate it).
- Use your own name on all credit applications (Mrs. Dick Levin *won't* do; Charlotte Levin *will*).
- Keep your own credit if you marry (or do it for the second or third time, too, when you take his name); all you do here is notify all of your creditors that you intend to maintain your own credit separate from your husband's regardless of the fact that you are taking his last name.
- Go to another bank or financial institution if you feel you've been discriminated against.
- Make a financial institution give you (in writing) the reasons why your credit application was rejected.
- Get a lawyer if you think you are being jerked around.
- If you want to start something bigger, write or call the state banking commissioner and explain what has happened to you.
- If you are just not credit-worthy (and you'll know this in your heart of hearts), don't get involved in a discrimination suit, just consider marrying money! Or maybe even starting a new religion.

WHY YOU NEED MORE THAN ONE BANK

Here I've already written more than sixteen pages about checking out deals, calculating what interest rates they are charging (or paying), and even why you should switch banks (and file a complaint I hope too) when you believe things are not fair. In each instance, it's been assumed there *is* another place to go, another bank that *is* willing to have your business (and on terms more favorable to you, too), a financial institution out there that *will* give you a better deal—or at least something to use as a comparison. It's just like trading cars! If you walk into the first showroom you stop at, hear their "best" deal, write them a check (or sign a note), and drive out with your new car, you deserve whatever you get. If you make three or four stops, get each person's very best deal in writing (always in writing with car salespersons and bankers) and *then* choose, you are doing it right.

But you say, how can I do business with more than one bank, and should I? Yes, you should, and here's why. There's no time quite as bad as when you've been turned down by your *only* bank, just at a time you need them the most, and you face the prospect of a cold turkey call on another bank (or a collect call home to someone, maybe) when your "bargaining power" is lowest. Here's why you need two banks:

- To keep one more option open at all times
- So you don't have to take the first bank's last and final deal
- So you can get some good old-fashioned free enterprise competition going between your banks (interest rates, fees)
- So you can have some time to "maneuver" (shop for a better deal)
- So you never run out of money
- So your financial fortunes are never at the mercy of just one individual

You *should* shop for money with *no* need to feel sensitive about it. Your liquidity is much too important to leave to one banker. And when you are shopping, remember these few home truths about banks:

- Getting a loan at one percent less interest is not a good deal *if* you have to agree to onerous terms (too much collateral, too little time to repay it, jeopardy to other assets you own). If necessary, it's better to pay a percent or two more for a better "total" financial deal. You never die from percents.

- If your supportive, friendly, empathetic banking officer moves to another bank in your city, consider moving with her. She knows you and you have trained her, and that's the stuff good banking relationships are made of.
- Don't be reluctant to let the first banker know you do business with another bank—how else does competition work?
- Remember this: Even if you forget everything else I said about banking, everything in a bank is negotiable if you find the right person.

I HAVE THIS BANKER FRIEND WHO ADVISES ME

It may seem natural to believe that an intelligent banker who is able to lend money, count money, collect money, deal with business people, and do all this at a profit would be a great investment adviser for you to line up. Not so! Your banker gets real good at taking in your money at one rate and lending it out again at a higher rate, but generally that's it! Her competence beyond getting and lending is neither highly developed nor especially objective given how she earns her salary. And that disqualifies her from acting as a financial adviser. Friend, maybe; lender, surely; collector, you bet your life. But adviser on how to accumulate wealth? No way!

REPRISE

Banks—we need them to get where we want to be. We need more than one and we need to shop hard for everything we "buy" from them too! Watch out for hidden charges and deals that feather the bank's nest, and don't ever sign anything without reading it twice. Remember that they sell money, and like toothpaste companies, they advertise hard to sell their share. Don't fall for the doric columns, the pinstripes, the sincerity, and the ads. Negotiate—with more than one. Pay a few dollars more interest to get more flexible terms.

7

You and the Experts

I don't want a lawyer to tell me what I cannot do; I hire him to tell me how to do what I want to do. J. P. MORGAN

TIME AND DISTANCE

Everyone has a couple of personal definitions of the term *expert.* I once heard it said that an expert was anyone more than seventy-five miles from home. My favorite definition of an expert is someone who borrows your watch so he can tell you what time it is. As a consultant, I often get ribbed along these lines, but less so since I bought my own Seiko and quit working near Chapel Hill.

An expert has just three things to offer you:

- An objective, unbiased view of your problem
- Sufficient technical knowledge to solve such problems
- The intelligence to reason through your problem with you.

In the event that one or more of these qualities is missing, forget it. That kind of an "expert" will be of little value to you, and may in fact hurt you.

Of course, the problem comes in testing whether these qualities are present. Each of us "experts" dresses in our professional finery, masters our own persuasive language, and behaves as if we can deliver exactly what you want. Licensing of professionals is old hat for CPAs and lawyers, but is still in its infancy regarding financial advisers. *The Wall Street Journal* (December 2, 1985) reported, in fact, that the largest U.S. association of financial planners awarded membership as a certified financial planner to a dog named Boris Bo Regaard, of Tampa, Florida. This of course makes it difficult for us to put a lot of credence in "diplomas." CPAs and lawyers are screened as to technical competence by organized "licensing" societies, and to a lesser extent as to intelligence by virtue of the protracted university experience they must undergo, but even that is imperfect. Screening them for their ability to deliver an objective unbiased view falls to you and me to do ourselves.

Nor is income or fees charged a consistent measure of objectivity, technical knowledge, or intelligence. *Time* magazine reported in August 1986 that one New York City law firm was now offering new law school graduates $65,000 as a starting salary, an hourly cost to the hiring law firm of about $30; in turn, it is common for such firms to bill these new employees out to clients for hourly rates up to $100—a stunning applied example of "buy low, sell high." It would be difficult to persuade a whole lot of thinking people that a freshly minted lawyer is "worth" $65,000 right out of the chute, but so much for the vagaries of labor markets.

In creating wealth, it is often necessary to make use of experts, and as much as I may poke some honest fun at them, you and I must still get to the point where (1) we decide whether we need expert help, (2) we decide which category of expert can help us, and (3) we interview and select someone to fill that bill. To do less makes us vulnerable!

In this chapter, we'll take a look at four kinds of experts who may have a role in your wealth-creation strategy:

- CPAs
- Lawyers
- Brokers
- Financial advisers

(We've already picked on bankers enough, and we'll wait till Chapter 13 to pick on insurance agents.)

We'll examine what these experts do, who they do it for, what they charge, what their agenda is, how to decide whether you need one, and what you might consider in choosing one. We'll assume you *do* have a watch!

CERTIFIED PUBLIC ACCOUNTANTS

In a heated argument with a CPA (not mine) some years back, I declared that I was convinced he *was* "certifiable." Charlotte says I don't get that abusive any more, but this particular tax adviser's statements persuaded me that he was in the employ of the I.R.S., a transposition of loyalties that absolutely baffled me.

Those who know me would tell you that I am doctrinaire about very few things. I have an intense dislike of warm beer, an absolute revulsion for lima beans, and a short fuse with those who are genetically programmed never to answer a question with "yes" or "no." But in the positive column of dogmas, add this: Most folks who read this book can benefit financially from finding themselves a good accountant. That's dogma? Yes, really. I'm not out here pimping for the accounting trade, but given what the reasonable ones charge, you can make money by using one (the right one, of course) when it comes to your wealth and tax matters. And you know how I feel about your wealth creation and tax avoidance.

I have had three accountants as advisers (not at the same time—I *do* trust folks) over the last twenty years—that period of my life when I have focused on wealth creation. Each of the three relationships was a strong one, and each time we parted friends. Go ahead and ask me—don't be timid—why three, then, Dick? As you and I move through the "stages" of our own wealth creation strategy, our needs for accounting and tax advice change. It's sort of like your kids "graduating" from their pediatrician to an "adolescent doctor" to an internist. For a few years, I did my own tax work and filled out my tax forms; after all, I was a college graduate and could read the Form 1040 instructions. Besides, if you want the truth, my income was so paltry that errors of consequence were nearly impossible—something about 20 percent of zero is still zero.

At the point where Charlotte and I bought our first piece of investment real estate (not a big deal at all—a duplex I'll tell you more about in Chapter 11, on which we put a $2,000 down payment), I got a CPA friend of mine to help me with the taxes—not so that he could read the Form 1040 instructions to me, but so that he could explain what to do about the duplex. When I think back at the paltry sums he charged me, the taxes he saved me, the stupid mistakes I would likely have made had I done it myself, and the time it gave me for fishing (and buying more duplexes), it was the best deal going at the time! Joe (that's what we'll call him) was a good "duplex" accountant. He knew how to figure depreciation (however, he preferred to use the method that at that time helped the I.R.S. the most—called straight line), and his work was neat, on time, and oh *so* conservative! In the five years that we worked together, I know I overpaid the I.R.S., but at the time I really didn't know enough to know it (if you know what I mean). By any measure, though, Joe was still a big bargain over what probably would have happened if I had tried to do it all myself.

Joe gave way to Harry, who not only knew what to do with duplexes (there were more by then) but also understood tax deferrals, partnership losses, and other more complex tax deals that Charlotte and I were into by then. Harry was a good bit more liberal than Joe (he knew what "gray" meant in tax terminology). Harry had only two faults: (1) he was not knowledgeable about the nuances of tax-deferred pensions for the self-employed (neither was I), and (2) he was unable to compute for me half a dozen or so different versions of my projected tax return (using different treatments of certain income and expense items) so that I could "test" which one generated the lowest income tax. Harry was a real gentleman and a hell of a bargain; he just became obsolete, given the stage of wealth creation I was then in.

My current coach is J. R. (his real name is Dick but his initials are J. R.). He understands duplexes and all the other stuff my other two friends knew, but he eliminates the two shortcomings of Harry: (1) he "wrote the book" on tax-deferred pensions for the self-employed (he even has his own lawyer and actuary to do the fancy words and numbers), and (2) his computer is able to spit out a quick dozen variations of my tax return to let me see where the smallest bite will be. J. R. is very professional, very liberal (with the IRS's money), very parsimonious with mine, always on time (you *never* have to call him, he always calls you), and, God willing, we will be together for a couple more decades at least! Moral: As your needs change, your need for advice changes. If you can find one CPA who can provide for your needs throughout your entire wealth-creation period, and you can learn to love each other, great! If not, shop, shop, and shop some more till you find a match! It's your money, and as your money matters get more and more complex, it's harder and harder (and dumber and dumber too) to be your own tax adviser! Oh, yes—stay away from tax services that will do it for $10 (state return included). That may be the worst free lunch you ever ate!

HENRY VI

I know this developer who has an enormous sign on his wall right above his desk with the famous line from Shakespeare's *Henry VI:* "The first thing we do, let's kill all the lawyers." Now regardless of what lawyers have or haven't done to my developer, I think that's unfair! My lawyer, "Skip," guided me around the rocks (and some sharks, too) for years until he died. He read all the fine print before I signed anything, he counseled me readily and thoughtfully by phone, he had boundless good common sense, he didn't gossip at cocktail parties, and he was completely honest. He was unbeatable! I think everyone with wealth creation in mind needs a "Skip"—not necessarily someone in a big fancy office you make appointments with, but someone you pick up the phone and call (on the spot) to see if you are getting ready to do something dumb, illegal, or dangerous, someone you may pay only a couple hundred dollars a year in fees for the phone calls, or more for contracts and closings. Skip was exactly that kind of person, a telephone friend with a great practical sense of the law. Skip persuaded me of that years ago when he defined "the law" to me one day. I was arguing with him that I had a "can't-lose" situation under the law. "Dick," he said, "the law is what some judge *says* it is on a Wednesday at 3 o'clock." How could I lose with an adviser like that! Are you listening, Skip? Get one—nuff said!

BROKERS

Back about six years ago, Roger R. Wilson, whom many of you will remember as the star of two raunchy movies, *Porky's* and *Porky's II,* claims that he placed over $2,000,000 in an account with a major Wall Street brokerage house for them to invest for him. His legal complaint alleges that about two years later the value of his account was a bit over *one dollar.* Don't panic. This case is an exception, but a good way to start this section, wouldn't you agree?

In point of fact, most folks in the brokerage business work pretty hard (for you too) and try to make you money (them too though). The bottom line probability is nearly zero that the average broker will make you rich, however. In fact, your chances of doing it yourself by making your own successful buy and sell decisions are about as good as the average broker's. Like everything else, there are always exceptions, but when you look at it over more than ten years, the assertion we make is a correct one! A word to the wise!

IRA, THE EXECUTOR

My cousin Ira (whose birthday in October is the same date as the enabling legislation for the federal income tax) is a good broker. Ira sees himself basically as an "executor," not an advice-giver or a salesman. If you want to blow your whole fortune on Acme Crab-Pickers, Ltd., common stock, Ira will buy it for you. He won't be real happy inside, but he'll keep his mouth shut and buy it nonetheless. If you want to put all your wealth into U.S. Government T-bills, Ira will arrange that, too. He is very bright, hopelessly honest, and is the only person I know in the whole world who can watch three basketball games on television simultaneously. Ira will never try to talk you into what he is buying for himself, nor will he churn your account for the commissions. If you *ask* him what he thinks salaried folk who don't believe in the tooth fairy and who have lower than average stock market IQs ought to buy, he'll steer you into very safe, modest yield stuff: conservative mutual funds, government agency trusts, government-backed mortgages, and the like, but *never* the hottest penny stock on the entire Gulf coast, Acme Crab Pickers, Ltd. Ira is your ideal broker for folks who earn salaries and who want to keep some.

During the time when I dabbled in stocks, my broker's name was Alfred. Alfred, unlike Ira, had a hundred good deals on the tip of his tongue every day and a hundred dollars in his personal bank account. He was personable, aggressive, supremely self-confident (he was often wrong but never in doubt), and never put off by rejection. Alfred was the worst "stock picker" I ever met, but we did business successfully for years! Alfred and I had just *one* rule: The first time he called *me*, I got a new broker. Alfred understood. It worked like a charm!

Brokers all get paid on commission, just like kids who deliver newspapers; if you cancel the paper, the kid's cash flow suffers. Brokers make money when you are buying or selling, but not at *any* other time! Therefore, it is in their best interest for you to be buying or selling. There are only 10,985 ways to get you to buy or sell. And when she has you on the phone touting $5,000 of one of the brokerage firm's products, "R and D Technology Fund," for your account, don't expect her to be so forthcoming to note that if she sells her quota of this item, she and her "main squeeze" will spend a weekend at the Hyatt on Maui free! Caveat emptor—caveat investor, too!

Moral: Everyone who intends to use stocks (over my strong objection), bonds, mutual funds, or the hundred and forty other instruments available today to help create wealth needs a broker they can trust! The trick is finding someone who shares *your* wealth accumulation strategy. If you're sure you can make a million in one year on Acme Crab Pickers, Ltd., call Alfred; if you have more common sense and a firm grasp on reality, find an Ira. More about what brokers do and to whom in Chapter 12.

MEET BO REGAARD

I was serious when I told you earlier that one of the largest associations of financial planners admitted a dog named Bo! There's a pungent moral in that tale somewhere. The number of

financial planners in the U.S. today is somewhere between 50,000 and 250,000; we have to guess because they aren't licensed. They don't have to meet uniform registration requirements, so no one really knows how many of them there are. What is generally conceded, however, is that financial planners are the fastest-growing expert group in the country!

When financial planning is done right, it can be a real catalyst to your accumulation of wealth. When it's done poorly, it can bankrupt you. Unfortunately for the profession, the number of stories about financial advisers who have ruined clients is far greater than those about financial advisers who have made clients rich. Most financial advisers are sincere; they really do want to help. It's their knowledge and their methods that are often called into question. There isn't a state attorney general in the U.S. who isn't investigating financial advisers today, but take heart, there isn't a state medical society that isn't investigating physicians either. And the same holds true for lawyers and pharmacists, too.

Why is the field so popular? There are more people making more money today than probably at any other time in history. There are also more products for sale today than in the past (a product is a particular mutual fund or a particular tax-free bond fund), so more people feel they need a guide through the mine field. Also, there is a lot more attention being paid to retirement and creating retirement income these days, given the aging of the population. All of these forces create a fertile (and sometimes gullible) market for financial advice. When you realize that about 22 million U.S. households have earnings between $20,000 and $70,000, it makes for a big (and profitable) segment!

BO GETS PAID BY . . .

Financial advisers make their money in three ways: (1) strictly by fees, (2) strictly by commissions on the "products" they sell, and (3) a combination of items 1 and 2. A fee-only financial adviser usually charges a fee per year and touts herself as totally objective (since she doesn't sell a product). Such fees can be anywhere between $200 and $20,000 the first year but tend to drop in succeeding years. I have a friend whose entire portfolio amounts to less than $45,000 and who is an inveterate speculator in wildly fluctuating stocks; he pays his financial adviser $250 a year to sit by and watch the carnage. Probably somewhere near 10 percent of all financial advisers are of the fee-only genre. This includes accountants.

Commission-only advisers don't charge you for the advice (or for a financial plan if they suggest one for you); they make their money off the commissions on the products you buy. The benefit here is that you won't get hit with an expensive annual fee, but the "free lunch" you get is that some of these advisers push the products they handle, *not* financial planning.

Most financial advisers are of type 3, fee *and* commission, but with the bulk of their incomes coming from commissions, not fixed annual fees. Such advisers will generally tell you that as long as they disclose fully what their commissions are, there is, in their minds, no conflict of interest in this arrangement. They'll also try to persuade you that they represent a "single stop" financial supermarket, where you not only get your financial planning, but also the products to implement it without even cranking up your car.

MASS CONFUSION

There are associations of financial advisers everywhere. These and some universities grant a whole list of official-sounding certifications. Furthermore, those in the profession still can't agree on what financial planning is, who should do it, what training they ought to have, and whether planning should be divorced from "selling" product. Add the fact that financial planning today is offered by everyone from major investment banking houses to large national private financial planning companies (one with more than a hundred thousand in its salesforce) to your bookkeeper friend next door, and what you get is a mess (an amalgam, if you are not a cynic).

Marketing techniques used by this group range from junk mail (I must get half a dozen pieces touting financial planning every week) to unsolicited phone calls (generally just at the time you are sitting down to eat dinner) to "free" seminars. My own special punishment (as a professor) is a never-ending series of phone calls from former students, most of them nice kids, but some of them who had trouble mastering compound interest when they were here, assuring me that if I will just let them into my office for thirty minutes, they will make me rich. Rich I don't want to be—left alone I do!

SO WHAT SHOULD I DO, COACH?

I staked myself out earlier in this chapter by saying that you should get a CPA to help you with your taxes, and that you will benefit financially if you do. There are just too many nuances in the tax code for you to survive profitably by yourself. Then I told you that you need a lawyer you trust who you can call from time to time; I believe that's a money-maker and trouble-saver too. Finally, I pointed out that wealth creation will probable require you to purchase a financial instrument (you know what that is by now) at some time or other, so that a broker with a one-way-only phone is a good idea too.

And now we are down to whether you need a financial adviser. I know you are not going to accept some mush-headed, mealy-mouthed equivocation for an answer and you know me well enough by now to know that's not my style. So here it comes: The answer is *no,* assuming you meet this short handful of criteria:

- You are an objective person.
- You understand everything in this book.
- You do not believe in the financial tooth fairy.
- You are honest with yourself.
- You have enough personal discipline to carry out a plan.
- You are not afraid of looking ignorant, doing something different from your parents, or making mistakes now and then.

PLUSSES AND MINUSES

So what *can* the experts do for you—and what can they *never* do for you? The can-do list looks just as it did on the first page of this chapter with the addition of another item or two by now:

- An objective unbiased view of your problem (if you pick the right person; more on how to do that in a minute)
- Sufficient technical knowledge to suggest solutions (most experts *do* have this much training)
- The intelligence to reason through your problem *with* you (again, there are very few idiots in the "expert" business)
- Access to up-to-date information on laws, products, companies, and economic trends (a good business school library has the same material)
- The backup support provided by other staff experts in the expert's company (sometimes avoids your reinventing the wheel)

On the other hand, even the world's best experts can't:

- See your goals as clearly as you do (or as you ought to)
- Know your family as well as you do (I hope)

- Provide discipline when you have none (at least not legally they can't)
- Supply judgment that's any better than yours (we've assumed all the way from page one that you're a smart person)
- Make decisions for you (law and common sense both suggest you are the expert here)
- Know you as well as you know yourself

All things considered, the answer comes out *yes* for a CPA, a lawyer, and a broker (the executor type, please), and *no* for a financial adviser.

WHAT QUESTIONS TO ASK

Let's start with your CPA: relevant things you need to know before you make a deal with one include:

- Is she a liberal or a conservative with respect to tax matters?
- Does she know the meaning of "gray" in tax considerations?
- Can she respond to your needs in an organized, timely, consistent fashion?
- Is she interested in doing more than filling out your tax return?
- Can she be reached by telephone fairly easily and will she mind responding using that medium?
- Is she discreet with private information?
- What has been the audit experience of her clients? (If they never get audited, drop her—she'll give the I.R.S. your money.)
- Is she smooth with I.R.S. auditors—unflappable?
- What research background does she have with respect to keeping abreast of changes in statutes?
- Is she really interested in small clients or looking to build a corporate practice?
- Is she honest?

- Will she give you a list of half a dozen of her current clients and one or two who have dropped her?
- Does she come across as bright?

The list for lawyers would include such things as:

- Does he appear to be interested in you and your plans?
- Did he ask you questions about your family and their part in your strategy?
- Is your lawyer reasonably well-connected in the community and in the profession?
- Does your bank think well of this attorney?
- Does he return phone calls on time?
- Does he talk too much at cocktail parties?
- Is his practice mainly corporate or mostly folks like you?
- Does he respond with "yes" or "no," or does he tend to equivocate?
- Does he give you the feeling sometimes that you are doing something illegal?
- Does he look like he'd be tough in negotiating for you or a pushover?
- Will he give you a client list of folks like you to call for references?
- Does he keep appointments on time?
- When you walk in his office, has he read your file yet?

The list for brokers is even smaller:

- Does she work for a discount brokerage firm? (This is the only way you can save about half the cost of brokerage services, unless a full-rate broker consistently shares her commissions with you, an event with the frequency of Halley's comet.)
- Does she consistently call you up cold, touting company products? (A yes is a quit signal.)

- Does she have at least five years' experience? (With some exceptions, less is bad.)
- Will she get you research information on something *you* are interested in quickly?
- Will she keep you current on all developments affecting "products" you currently own?
- Will she give you the names of at least three clients she's lost?
- Will she let you manage your own wealth?

Financial advisors get a very very short list:

- Forget them (but read the list of criteria on page 125 again first).

WRAP

Surrounding yourself with a small cadre of experts you feel comfortable with (and who help you get where you want to be in this business of creating wealth) is not a particularly easy thing to do. Like marriage, it will require lots and lots of accommodation and may even end in a divorce or two! So be it. There are at least a quarter of a million experts in each technical category and one of them is right for you! But as you go through the process of acquiring and retaining your own little cadre, remember that your role is *making* the decisions. Their role is advising, pointing out holes in the road (or rocks under the water so you can appear to walk on it from time to time), carrying out your decisions, and keeping you out of jail. And when you find your Ira, your Alfred, your J. R. (and your own Charlotte, my *best* expert), it'll feel right. That's how you'll know.

8

Deals That Are Really Hard to Beat (IRAs, Keoghs, Company-matching Deals)

It's wonderful per se. CHIEF JUSTICE EARL WARREN

YES, VIRGINIA, THERE ARE FINANCIAL SANTA CLAUSES

Who among us hasn't at least found a dime on the street—all right, a penny then? And who hasn't gotten at least one of those small free samples of shampoo, deodorant soap, or miracle laundry detergent in the mailbox unsolicited? Even the most cynical of us sometimes turn hypocritical when we load up our suitcase with shampoo, soap, sewing kits, and hair conditioner provided by those "higher-quality motels." Teetotalers who fly first class have been known to order "two scotches unopened please with no chaser" to take home and display or serve to guests—*four* when the plane makes an intermediate stop.

Yes, the world does have its bitesize free-lunch samples, and the world of finance is no exception either. It's not the case that companies stand around and give away their assets for no good reason or that the federal government gives away great tax deals willy-nilly. But if you look closely at some of the benefits your company offers you (in exchange, of course, for your undying loyalty and hyperproductivity for the next thirty-five years) you'll occasionally find a small free lunch. And when you find one, you should eat it with gusto!

The feds give away these little nearly-free lunches too, but not for either your loyalty or productivity—more because enough politicians think it gets them votes without bankrupting the government. Cynical, yes, but true too! Federal nearly-free lunches taste at least as good as company ones. (Unless some fat cat eats them, in which case we call them outrageously-free lunches, a.k.a. loophole—and lobby for tax reform.)

Company-sponsored nearly-free lunches generally take the form of "matching actions"; that is, the company says to you "For every dollar you put into this savings plan, we'll put in fifty cents." Or if you work for a Scrooge outfit, it's "You put in a dollar, we put in a dime." Nevertheless, Scrooge or not, it's a free bite of lunch, and only a fool turns down his or her dime. Unless, of course, the deal is that you have to invest your dollar (and their dime) in a company stock, which you can't touch for fifty years or until your oldest male child has three female offspring, two of which have worked for the company for at least twenty years. (Maybe I was right—there's *no* free lunch.)

Government free bites for you and me are a bit different. Since 1776, Washington hasn't come around saying that if you buy $100 worth of government bonds, they will chip in another $25 free—oh no. But they *do* allow you to make some investments that you can deduct (now *there's* a word we like) from your taxable income this year, and on which you can accumulate interest, tax-free (there's *another* nice word) until you start drawing the money out from whatever you have it invested in. Of course, there's a lot more to it than what I just wrote (lots and lots of conditions, "whereases," limitations, and penalties), but the nearly-free lunch *is* there for the taking, if you know how to shop a menu.

This chapter focuses on nearly-free lunches, both the private and government kinds. It's our first chapter on investing, and it belongs first too. If someone lines up a lot of lunches in front of you with price tags, and they are of similar food value but widely different prices (I didn't say ambiance, taste, appearance, or smell—I said *food value*; after all, money *is* money) and you pick the most expensive one over the free one, then you are either dumb or rich. In either case, you won't benefit much from this book. On to nearly-free lunches then!

SPONSORING FRUGALITY—DIFFERENT VIEWS

A lot of the business tycoons of the past three centuries believed in frugality. Some of them demonstrated this by paying their employees less than it took them to live, thereby getting rich off their labors. Both Dickens and Marx wrote at length of this common practice. Other more enlightened employers sponsored employees' frugality by encouraging savings, doing this by contributing something themselves (sometimes called "matching," although the annals of history are hardly replete with examples of 100 percent matching of employees' savings)—i.e., contributing a certain percentage of whatever the employee decided to save. Thus, if the company put in their twenty-five cents for each dollar you decided to save, you accumulated money in your savings account (or theirs) at a rate twenty-five percent faster than you would have without the company contribution. This was not only a company's encouragement of good financial habits, but clearly an early employee benefit. Since this practice began long before income tax laws (recall that was 1913 in the United States), the whole deal was not contaminated with before-tax, after-tax, marginal-tax-rate mumbo-jumbo. Of course, way back then, not too many people could afford to save a whole lot, and the monies accumulated in these kinds of plans were not enormous.

Nevertheless, look around you and see if your company sponsors one of these plans. Many companies still offer these savings or "thrift" plans, under which you authorize them to deduct some proportion of your pay to be invested in a "qualified" savings plan. "Qualified" refers to the restrictions the feds put on you about what you do with the money, for how long, and what happens when you leave your employer. The company agrees to supplement your contribution by a certain percentage of their own (somewhere between 0 and 100 percent). Here's an example: If you earn $35,000 and the maximum amount you can invest in such a plan is 10 percent of your salary, and if the company agrees to match you dollar for dollar up to 20 percent of your own contribution, the arithmetic goes like so:

You earn per year	$35,000	
You deduct per year	3,500	(10% of $35,000—a lot of VCR's, vacations, and beer)
The company adds per year	$700	(20% of $3,500)
You accumulate per year	$4,200	($3,500 plus $700)

For fun, let's assume you invest $4,200 every year at 8 percent for twenty years. The total money you would have at that time would be $207,576, a princely sum for a modest assumed interest rate of 8 percent; but the real deal here is that of that amount, the company has contributed $34,596. (If you're a little rusty on doing these numbers, go back and reread Chapter 4.)

Worth looking around again, isn't it? If your company has such a plan, and if the restrictions they put on what you can do with the money aren't too onerous, you might want to "max-out." Freely translated, that means borrow on the house, the car, the kids, and your spouse's inheritance to take advantage of it. The company's contribution is nothing less than a gift from them, and one that puts you on the road to wealth accumulation faster, quite apart from a possible tax advantage (which we shall discuss shortly). Suffice it to say that the more you do of this, the more wealth you will be able to accumulate. On the other hand, for every dollar you put into this deal, you have to give up spending a dollar today on goodies such as vacations, VCRs, a new car, clothes, and beer. That may be what people mean when they say "There ain't no free lunch."

ENTER SAM

The federal government got into the act in an effort to stimulate citizens to save for their own retirement. After all, if you've looked at the social security that you (and your spouse if you are married) will draw when you're too old to work (or too smart), it's frightening. You just can't live on $567.81 a month, or at least you can't live very well on $567.81 a month. So, some years ago, the federal government began to concentrate on methods to encourage people (either with their company's support or by themselves) to supplement their social security. Voilà! A whole new set of fancy numbers (referring to sections and paragraphs of the tax code), names, and deals. The government's effect on saving (and investing) for retirement is principally through the tax benefits they allow us when we get involved. These range all the way from the best deal—paying no tax until you begin withdrawing it (and there's the third nice word "no tax") on the *total amount* of money you take out of your earnings and put in a government-sanctioned savings plan (including interest)—to their worst deal—paying no tax only on the *interest* that accumulates in that retirement fund. But even the feds' *worst* deal in this instance is a *good* deal for you.

REMEMBER THE RULE: ALWAYS START WITH THE BEST DEAL

The absolute best deal the U.S. Government ever concocted for you was the IRA, Individual Retirement Account. In fact, it was too good and they watered it down with the 1986 revision to the tax law. Congress originally designated IRAs to give folks who didn't have a company pension plan a big incentive to save and start one. In 1981, they liberalized the law so that any full-time or part-time employee with or without a pension plan could start an IRA. In 1986, they scaled it back substantially, but it is still worth your careful consideration.

Until 1986, any individual could contribute up to $2,000 of income to an individual retirement account and deduct the $2,000 from taxable income—that's right, not pay tax on the $2,000 you invested in your own retirement (or the interest you earned on it either). And you could do that every year, even if you did not itemize other deductions. See why I labeled this the "best deal the U.S. Government ever concocted for you"?

But the Lord giveth and the Lord taketh away, and so too the government. Today, if neither you nor your spouse is covered by an employer's retirement plan (or a pension plan, as some folks like to call it), you can still claim a $2,000 deduction from your taxable income, regardless of how much money you make. Two-income couples without any retirement plan coverage by either employer are allowed two IRA deductions a year, or $4,000. A couple with just one income and no employer's retirement plan can claim a $2,250 deduction from their taxable income. This money and the interest it earns is allowed to accumulate without your paying any tax on it until you decide to draw it out. If you start drawing it out before you are 59 1/2 years old, the government charges you a penalty. Finally, you *must* begin drawing it out when you are 70. Then, whenever you withdraw it, you pay the federal tax on whatever you draw out that year at the current tax rate. That's a bit of a dice roll on your tax rates, but then the rates have trended down for most of your lifetime, so it's a better than even bet they won't go back up too much.

Why is this such a terrific deal for those who are not covered by a pension plan? Two reasons: First, it provides resources to supplement your social security (you really *can't* live on $567.81 a month social security), and second, the tax break you get is terrific. Not only do you accumulate interest on your investment tax-free (actually using the language of Chapter 5, you "defer" taxes, since ultimately they must be paid), you also get to deduct the actual $2,000 you put in the IRA from your taxable income. Here's some arithmetic to show why it's still the best thing going (for those not otherwise covered by a retirement plan):

Let's say you and your spouse earn $40,000 together after tax deductions	$40,000
Under the 1986 tax law revision, you'd pay 28% in tax which without IRAs would be	11,200
With an IRA for each of you, you'd deduct $4,000 from your taxable income which makes it	36,000
And the tax on this would be	10,080

You save $11,200 − 10,080, or $1,120, a year on taxes alone, plus you get to accumulate the whole thing ($4,000 a year for the both of you) plus the interest it earns, and not pay a penny of tax until you start using the money. If you really like numbers, look at it this way:

1. The two of you invested $4,000 a year.
2. You saved $1,120 in taxes.
3. And you can probably earn 8 percent on your $4,000 without much risk, which is $320 a year.
4. So putting it all together, you earned

$$\frac{\$1{,}120 \text{ plus } \$320}{\$4{,}000} \times 100\% = \text{a 36\% return}$$

(better than IBM!)

Of course, you are postponing doomsday on paying taxes, but as long as you can earn 36 percent and not pay the tax on it for years and years to come, do it, do it, do it!

BUT OUR COMPANIES HAVE PENSION PLANS, COACH

Ah, some sadness! But all is not lost. If *either one* of you is covered by a retirement plan where you work, and your adjusted gross income before deducting the $4,000 for the IRAs is less than $40,000 (joint return) or $25,000 (individual return), you can still play by the pre–1986 rules; yes, you can deduct the whole contribution ($4,000) from your taxable income. And we already know that earns you 36 percent on your money (tax-deferred, of course). And you can accumulate the interest your IRAs earn tax-free until you start taking out money—*defer* the tax, that is!

Hold on, there's more! If your adjusted gross income (you and spouse together) is between $40,000 and $50,000, or if your individual adjusted gross income is between $25,000 and $35,000, you can claim a *partial deduction*. The rule goes roughly like this: "For every dollar of income over $40,000 on a joint return (or over $25,000 on an individual return), your IRA deductions are reduced 20 cents. Thus, if your joint adjusted gross income is $45,000, that's $5,000 over $40,000, so your deduction for IRAs would be reduced:

20% × $5,000, or $1,000

which would cut it to $3,000 instead of the original $4,000. But that's still a good deal, because it still earns you a 36 percent return on the $3,000 (work it out as I did on page 136 if you are skeptical).

If you file individually, and your adjusted gross income is, say, $29,000, that's $4,000 over $25,000, and your IRA contribution would be reduced by:

20% × $4,000, or $800

which would make it $1,200 instead of the original $2,000. But not to fret—that's *still* a 36 percent rate of return (tax deferred, of course) and there aren't many investments in the world today (religion and drugs excluded) that make that kind of money! That's one reason why an IRA is the first investment you should consider.

If you are the kind of person who likes to play around with formulas, you'll soon find that if you lose 20 cents of deductibility for every dollar that your adjusted gross income is above $25,000 (individual filing), you lose your *whole $2,000 deductibility* by the time your individual income climbs to $35,000:

$$(\$35{,}000 - 25{,}000) \times 0.20 = \$2{,}000$$

but the feds in their mercy will still allow you a $200 IRA deduction as long as your income doesn't reach $35,000.

SO YOU EARN $35,000; HANG ON, ALL IS STILL NOT LOST

Even if your company has a pension plan, the feds will still let you invest $2,000 of your income in an IRA (individual filing), or $2,250 for a one-income couple, or $4,000 for a two-income couple filing jointly, and accumulate the interest it earns tax deferred until you draw it out. True, you can't deduct the contribution from your adjusted gross income as you did before, but you pay no tax on the *interest* you earn until you withdraw it. You've already paid the tax on the $2,000 deduction (or $2,250 or $4,000) when you invested it, so it isn't taxed again. Just the interest gets taxed this time. And before we leave this section, do you remember from Chapter 5 how to calculate what interest is worth when it's not taxed? To save you time, here's the formula from Chapter 5 again:

$$\text{Taxable equivalent yield} = \frac{\text{Tax-free yield}}{1 - \text{your tax rate}}$$

So, if you are paying 28 percent income tax and you get to invest your IRA money at, say, 7 percent without paying tax on the interest now, the taxable equivalent yield is:

$$\frac{7\%}{1 - 0.28}$$

or 9.722 percent. What does it mean? You can earn 7 percent investing in absolutely safe U.S. Government securities, so until you pay the interest, your taxable equivalent yield on this safest of all possible investments is almost 10 percent—not bad at all! And if you're 25 years old, it's a long time until you're 59 1/2! Who knows, by then they may have outlawed taxes.

INDUSTRIAL STRENGTH IRAs—WE CALL THEM 401(K)S

About ten years ago, Congress created a new section of the Internal Revenue Code, section 401(k), which permitted employees to designate a part of their salary as a contribution to a 401(k) tax-deferred retirement plan. It works just like the old (pre–1986 tax law) IRA, but has two major advantages:

1. Everything you contribute is still deductible from your taxable income (the contribution itself plus the interest).
2. The ceiling on contributions is roughly 20 percent of your earnings with a dollar maximum of $7,000. (I say "roughly 20 percent" because the code actually refers to "25% of compensation before 401(k) contribution," and I'd rather be roughly right than hunt around for an algebra book).

Contributions to a 401(k) tax-deferred retirement plan reduce your taxable income and thus your taxes. The interest your contributions earn over the years is not taxed either. You pay taxes on whatever you withdraw only when you retire. Sounds great, doesn't it?

One sticky point: The 20 percent of earnings in 401(k) contributions that you are permitted to set aside by federal law is the maximum. Your employer *can* set a lower limit on your contribution. And one nice point: Many employers match (up to a certain level) the contributions of their employees to 401(k) plans, so you get three nearly-free lunches—*first*, a lower taxable income by the amount you contribute and thus less tax; second, no tax on the interest your money earns until you withdraw it; and third, free contributions from your employer (if he or she participates) that are not taxed until you withdraw them for retirement years. All told, this is the best possible investment deal you can get.

One final word about 401(k)s: Generally, you can't take out the money you contribute until you die, retire, reach 59 1/2 years of age, become disabled, leave the company, or suffer financial hardship. What all this means is that unless you suffer a financial hardship, the feds will probably penalize you 10 percent on top of the tax you already owe on the money (which they will insist you pay). And what all that means is *don't* put money in a 401(k) retirement plan that you think you may need. It's a long time to 59 1/2 or death. Besides, if you earn 8 percent on the money and pay 10 percent in penalty, you have the whole thing backwards and, as you know by now, you cannot possibly create any wealth using that formula. It's kind of like buy high, sell low.

FOLKS LIKE ME GET TO PLAY TOO

Teachers, preachers, and those who work for many kinds of tax-exempt organizations get their own special section of the Internal Revenue Code—in this instance, section 403(b). It's sort of a 401(k) for us. Just like 401(k), neither the part of our income that we contribute to a tax-deferred retirement plan nor the interest that it earns is subject to federal income tax until it is withdrawn. Our maximum contribution is $9,500 a year. As you can imagine, very few teachers, preachers, or those who work for tax-exempt organizations can afford to contribute that much annually out of their salaries. Which just goes to prove that the rich get richer and the poor have more kids!

MISCELLANEOUS FREE LUNCHES

Many companies offer their employees group life, health, or disability insurance. Depending on a lot of factors, principally your age and health, it may be a terrific deal or a bummer. For example, if you're very young and in perfect health, you can get all kinds of cheap insurance yourself, in many instances cheaper than your company's group policy rates. Becoming a member of the group policy under those conditions doesn't pay. On the other hand, you may be nearly uninsurable because of age or health considerations, in which case becoming a group member is a real deal. Of course, if the company contributes all or a large part of the premium, sign whatever they put in front of you. Which reminds me of a story about a company with 100 employees that was offered a fantastic group life insurance policy under the condition that all 100 employees sign up. Ninety-nine signed up the first day, but one man held out for months, quarreling with every conceivable detail in the policy. Finally, the president called him into the office one morning and said, "Art, either sign this form or you are fired." He signed immediately. When he went back into the plant, his fellow workers asked him what had changed his mind about the policy. "Actually, it was very simple," he said. "No one ever explained it to me before."

WRAP

A nearly-free lunch is a nearly-free lunch is just *possibly*, a bona fide free lunch, be it food, money, lower interest rates, or lower tax rates. When you see one, grab it! It's as simple as that. Each of the opportunities we've covered in this chapter is either a free lunch or a bite of one. But taken as a whole, they are still the best investments for salaried men and women. Borrow against the house, sell your horse, mortgage your first born, or stop paying for sex—do whatever you must to make the maximum possible use of these vehicles—they are your best shot at wealth creation.

Finally, we haven't said anything here about *what* to invest these "freebies" in—just that you ought to take advantage of them. On now to some investment advice—where to put the goodies.

9

Safe Stuff—the Kind You Never Have to Worry About

The safest way to double your money is to fold it over once and put it in your back pocket. KIN HUBBARD

Never invest your money in anything that eats or needs repainting. BILLY ROSE

BLUEPRINT

This chapter is all about investments that are nearly risk-free—I say *nearly* because I too have read about such unlikely events as the sinking of the Titanic, the collapse of the Mackinaw bridge in Michigan, and the man who actually ate five watermelons at one time without dying. Nothing in life is without *some* risk, but on the great continuum of all possible investments, the ones we'll talk about here are way, way over on the low-risk side.

Of course, you always get what you pay for—and investing is no exception. Back in Chapter 2 ("Wealth Creation as a Mindset"), I introduced you to the notion of risk-return—that is, the more risk you are willing to take, the higher the return you can expect to earn. Or if you prefer the cynic's interpretation, the more return you think you are going to get, the more risk you are taking. Let me bore you for a minute with a repeat of an illustration we used there:

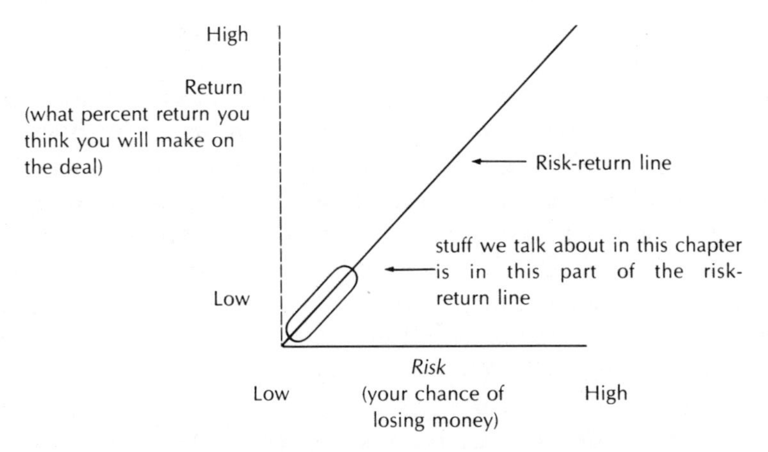

Figure 1 (repeated from Chapter 2)

All of the investments we will talk about in this chapter are down on the lower left-hand end of the risk-return line—the part I've circled in Figure 1. If investments of this type are your cup of tea, you can expect to earn a very modest rate of return; but in exchange for accepting that modest rate of return, the risk of losing your money is practically nil.

Some of your friends will scoff (some may actually call you old-fashioned or even wimpy) for accepting the modest return you get from investing in nearly risk-free alternatives, but when you bought this book you had already decided that you weren't a venture capitalist. And we've already made the case mathematically in earlier chapters that wealth creation doesn't depend on earning very high rates, but on persistence over time. So when someone calls you "awfully conservative," ask to see *his* balance sheet. Nuff said!

BACK TO THE BANK FOR A BEGINNING

Here's where you need to start. It's difficult to get along these days without one (better two) checking accounts. (Two let you move money around and be a little tougher; you remember we chatted about this in Chapter 6 too.) Here you keep (actually you invest because they pay interest now on checking accounts) enough money to get you through this month, but no more! To reinforce yourself on this point, go back and reread page 38 in Chapter 3. Banks pay very low rates of interest on monies kept in checking accounts, but in return your money is absolutely safe (as long as you have less than $100,000 in your account), even if the bank goes belly-up, which more and more seem to be doing these days. The Federal Deposit Insurance Corporation (FDIC) assures you that if the bank doesn't make it, any deposits less than $100,000 will be taken care of by Uncle Sam in due course—and it has worked so far. In the case of savings and loan associations, their guarantor is called Federal Savings and Loan Insurance Corporation (FSLIC).

Keeping more money in your checking account than you need to pay your monthly bills is not smart. There are just too many better alternatives. I notice that my bank will pay 5.13 percent on money in my checking account, and that my U.S. Government Treasury Bills (more about these later) are yielding 7.3 percent currently. Since the U.S. Government is a lot richer than my bank (it has to be if it's the organization that bails out the bank), I earn more every time I move money *out* of my bank! Of course, your bank will probably charge you something if your checking balance falls below a certain level (or at least charge you more for processing every check and deposit if that happens), but they can't make much of a living paying you 5.13 percent on your money and doing an enormous amout of bookkeeping, computerized recordkeeping, and mailing for you. Look at it this way: Suppose you keep only $100 in your checking account; the bank pays you $5.13 a year interest (my current rate); they do the accounting on your balance; they maintain computer records all of the time on you; they send you a statement every month and again at year end; and they provide someone at the other end of the phone to answer your calls and help you reconcile your bank balance if you need it—all for whatever *they* can earn on your $100. Not exactly their best shot at making their stockholders rich, is it? More about how to figure out these bank charges in a bit.

CHECKING AND SAVING—SAVING AND CHECKING

Big question—if you have a checking account do you need a savings account too? This issue should be decided strictly on the basis of financial return. Most savings accounts at banks (and savings and loans too) pay just a tad more interest than their checking accounts, something generally on the order of 1/4%. That's not much return for you to bother with two kinds of accounts, nor does the savings account offer you anything today that you can't get with your checking account. So the rule is don't bother with a savings account except in two instances: (1) if you don't have enough personal discipline to avoid spending more than the balance in your checking account, or (2) when little brother owns or runs the bank and is giving you side deals that are terrific—in that case, put the money wherever he says but watch what you sign! Final note: In the United States, folks have over $200 billion invested in passbook savings accounts, most of it at very low rates of interest. What that means is either these people know something I don't, I know something they don't, or one of us is crazy. You figure it out!

STEPPING UP AT THE BANK

If your checking account balance is anything over $500, the computer has no doubt singled you out from among thousands of depositors and sent you volumes of mail about "opportunities for higher yields." In other words, your bank wants you to invest some money with them that they know you can't withdraw for between 3 months and 3 1/2 years. That makes life easier for the bank's financial planners because they know your money will be right back there in the till every day. If you want to participate, they will give you a "certificiate of deposit," signifying that it *is* your money right back there in the till. And they will pay you a higher rate of interest too! What that rate is depends on how long you sign up to keep your money right back there in the till. If you're in for six months, the rate is generally about one percent more than what they pay you on your checking balance; if you sign up to leave it there for three years, the rate is generally about 2 1/2 percent more than the bank's checking account rate. Of course, you have your certificate of deposit (CD) and your interest every month, but not your money for three years, so here we go again, the Lord giveth and the Lord taketh away!

CDs are quite safe. The federal government insures that you will get your money back. If you *do*, however, need your money before the term of your contract runs out, the bank will penalize you (the feds *make* them do this) by reducing your earnings and assessing a penalty for early withdrawal. Investing in CDs requires you to do some financial planning to see how much you can afford to do without for what period of time. Absent this, you will pay a lot of penalties and earn a very low rate of return on your efforts. Finally, CDs can't be bought for a dollar a week; you have to invest a minimum amount—say $500—to get in on this deal. So unless you are rich, you have to use your checking account to "inventory" money until it amounts to enough to buy a CD—or as they say in Salter Path, North Carolina, (a village near where I fish in the summer): "Them as has gits." You can always tell when you are doing better financially—you begin to get more computer letters touting CDs.

ONE MORE STEP UP AT THE BANK

Most banks also offer "money market accounts." These are essentially savings accounts with the rate of interest tied to what's happening in the money market—that is, how interest rates are behaving across the country. When the interest rate goes up, you earn more; when it goes down, you earn less. Money market accounts pay higher interest rates than savings accounts and checking accounts too, but the rates fluctuate daily. Your bank may require a minimum deposit for you to open or add to one, and it may permit you to write checks on your money market account balance. Please don't confuse these with money market *mutual funds*, which are *not* insured by the federal government, but are private funds investing your money in various short-term loans to banks, governments, and private companies. We will discuss these further in a later chapter on riskier investments.

WHAT'S IT ALL ABOUT, ALFIE?

All of the bank investments we've noted are risk-free, that is, as we have said, all of them are insured by the federal government. Since all of them then have essentially the same risk (nearly zero), you, the investor, have to make a choice among them based on other criteria which are:

1. the interest rate they pay
2. how long you must give up the use of your money
3. what minimum level of deposit is required
4. what kinds of bank service charges you will pay (cost per

check written, cost per deposit, cost if your balance falls too low, etc.)

Picking and choosing on the basis of interest rates seems easy, but banks have computers, and consequently have been able to design thousands of different investment opportunities for you. If you are as serious about wealth creation as I think you are, the *only* way to compare is to use the quant-jock stuff that we introduced in Chapter 4. That's right, turn back to the tables there, sit down with your hand-held calculator, and figure out how much money you will have at the end of "X" years under all of the alternatives you are considering. Then pick the highest one if interest rates are your only consideration.

If having to give up your money for too long a time is a major consideration, then be ready to earn a bit less and keep your money invested for a shorter period. No computer can help you here. What you must do is decide what is the longest period of time you can do without the money, then pick the highest interest rate some bank will give you for investing for that long. That's a trade-off you have to make in your head, after carefully considering your personal financial situation (income, expenses, unforeseen purchases, etc.). The bank can't help you here at all!

Most people who earn what you do can get up the minimum level of deposit required for just about all of the bank investments we've covered. It varies between zero and about a thousand dollars, and for those who do a bit of financial planning, it is rarely the most potent criterion in choosing among bank investments—which of course leaves us with bank service charges and related deals. Here banks run wild with imagination, and that makes it more difficult to figure out who's on first. Listen to this recent deal from a Southeastern U.S. bank:

> If you have a passbook savings account, a money market account, or a checking account with us, you will receive 5/100% over our current 2 1/2 year CD rate. If you maintain $10,000 in your passbook savings account or in a CD, we will not charge you the usual $10 a month service charge on

your checking account. In addition, if you are under 18, you can open a money market savings account with less than our usual $500 minimum deposit and you don't have to keep our minimum required $500 balance in that account, if any member of your immediate family has any account at our bank.

HELP, ALFIE!

Not to fret. It's Machiavellian for sure, but like most conundrums, it will yield if you pick it apart piece by piece. Besides, if a banker thought it up, we can figure it out. Let's go. The easy part first: If you are over eighteen or an orphan, just forget the whole last part of the bank's deal about opening a money market savings account with less than the usual $500 deposit—that one was simple.

Now look at the part about waiving the service charge on your checking account. If you didn't pay the bank that, you'd save 12 × $10, or $120, a year. But what would you have to add to your passbook savings or CD to get it up to $10,000? If the answer is "nothing," then you save the $120—no sweat. If, however, you have no passbook savings account and only $8,000 in CDs, then you have to add $2,000 to your CD investment with the bank. Suppose you currently have $2,000 invested at say a 1 percent return over what the bank will pay you on a CD. Moving your $2,000 costs you 1% × $2,000, or $20 a year, but if you do this, you save the $120 service charge on your checking account—a good deal and $100 profit too!

Now to the first part of the bank's offer to you—5/100ths percent more interest on a 2 1/2-year CD if you have a passbook savings account, a money market account, or a checking account with them. If you do, you qualify automatically. If you don't, don't open a new account for a mere 5/100ths of a percent interest. Five one hundredths of a percent interest on $1,000 is only 50¢ a year, and you shouldn't do *anything* for 50¢ a year, much less open an account.

REPRISE ON BANK INVESTMENTS

Shop banks to compare interest rates, service charges, and minimum balances, and the time you are required to deposit your money with them. Don't be bashful—the bank money managers shop the international money market daily for bargains and you should too. Don't be bashful either about having a CD at one bank and a checking account at another—if it pays, do it! Pay no attention to bankers who say that they prefer that you have all of your bank relations with them—that's the bank's way of saying "We want to increase our market share in this city." And, finally, whatever you do, don't try to become an interest-rate forecaster. The federal government can't do it; company economists can't do it; your own bank can't do it; my colleagues at the university can't do it; and you can't do it either. Just invest what you can afford to invest at the highest rate you can get and for the longest time you can afford to be without the use of your money. Let it go at that. Don't chase your tail all over the county to earn an additional 5/100ths of one percent. And no regrets when rates move up three days after you've bought a CD. Have a beer and remember the *experts* who lost millions on October 19, 1987.

INVESTING IN UNCLE SAM IS RISK-FREE TOO

Your federal government offers a wide array of risk-free investments under five major categories:

1. Savings bonds
2. Treasury bills
3. Treasury notes
4. Treasury bonds
5. Obligations of various federal agencies.

Except for some of the federal agency obligations (more on them in a minute), all of these are guaranteed by the U.S. Government—about as close to risk-free as you can hope to get.

Consequently, none of these investments offers a real high

interest rate—you remember, no free lunch. But all of them offer rates comparable to bank CDs and money market accounts, and some of them don't require you to keep your money tied up as long as a CD.

Series EE Savings Bonds

These are probably the most ubiquitous government security ever offered. You buy these bonds at a discount from their face value, and their value increases throughout the period you hold them. The difference between purchase price and redemption value equates to the interest you earn. Maturity is usually five years and you don't pay taxes on the interest you are earning until the end of the five years. You also generally don't pay state or local income taxes on the interest either. You can buy these at any post office without a fee.

Treasury Bills

These are investments the U.S. Government offers to raise money to pay its current debts—those coming due within a year. These bills mature in three, six, or twelve months (actually thir-

U.S. GOVERNMENT SECURITIES

teen, twenty-six, and fifty-two weeks, since they are sold weekly). You can buy these through your bank. They are sold at a discount, and the difference between what you pay and what you cash them in for is your earned interest. You can sell them any day you want, but their value fluctuates according to interest rates, and the only way to guarantee getting your money and interest back is to hold them until they mature. One kicker is that you need a minimum investment of $10,000, which tends to make them unsuitable for investors with a modest salary until some wealth has been accumulated. Until that point, if you desire risk-free investments, use the bank. With T-bills, there's no state or local income tax on the interest you earn.

Treasury Notes

These mature in two to ten years and they pay interest semiannually at a guaranteed rate. You can sell them at any time, but if you decide to sell when interest rates are way up, your note is worth a lot less than what you paid for it. However, if you keep it until maturity, you get the entire face value back when you sell it. You buy these notes through a bank or your securities broker, and they are generally sold in amounts of $5,000, but the U.S. Treasury can reduce that minimum amount to $1,000 if it wants. Like the other U.S. Government securities, they are free of state and local income taxes.

Treasury Bonds

You can buy these bonds to mature in from ten to thirty years. Generally, they have the highest rate of interest of any of the U.S. Government securities that we've discussed; for example, today's 30-year bond rate is 8.7 percent and today's 13-week Treasury bill rate is about 6.2 percent. Of course, locking up your money for thirty years *should* be worth something. Aside from the different maturities, these bonds have the same characteristics as Treasury notes, including the fact that you pay no state or local income taxes. Like the notes, the interest is sent to you every six months. If you have to sell one of these at the end of ten years, say, and interest rates are way up over what they were when you bought it, it just won't be worth as much as it says on the face of it, and you'll eat the loss. But if you keep it to maturity and the U.S. Government is still in business here, you are home free—actually you are home risk-free!

OBLIGATIONS OF VARIOUS FEDERAL AGENCIES

All kinds of pieces and parts of the U.S. Government need to borrow money from you and me; some of these organizations are called "agencies" and their investments are available for us too. There are many choices here, some guaranteed by the government, some not, so you have to be careful if your game is risk-free investing! Some of the organizations offering securities are the Federal Intermediate Credit Bank, Government National Mortgage Association, Federal Home Loan Bank, and the Federal National Mortgage Association. For most of you, none of these agencies' securities represent any significantly better opportunity than the previously discussed government bills, notes, and bonds, except the Government National Mortgage Association securities called Ginnie Maes. These represent a chance to earn a somewhat higher rate than on government securities (often 2 percent or more higher), and since they are guaranteed by the U.S. Government, that should get our interest.

Ginnie Maes appeared in 1970; that year, Congress passed a law that allowed savings and loan associations, mortgage bankers and banks to "package up" mortgages that they had made, issue certificates, and sell these to the public to raise more money to lend on mortgages. The government guaranteed the certificates so they could be sold easily. If you buy one, it works like this: As the bank, S&L or mortgage banker collects the mortgage payments represented by the Ginnie Mae certificate, he passes your share through to you and that's how you get your money back (both interest and return of some principal comprise each payment). Safe, sound, all guaranteed!

Originally, you had to buy $100,000 worth of these, so they weren't too popular with the average Jill; then the minimum amount fell to $25,000; now you can buy them in practically any amount from brokerage firms that put together funds whose entire investment is in Ginnie Maes.

DOES IT REALLY MAKE ANY DIFFERENCE, ALFIE?

If the lowest rate we talked about in this chapter was the 5.13 percent my bank pays me on money in my checking account, and the highest rate we noted was the 8.7 percent on thirty-year Treasury bonds, is the difference enough to care about—or, as they say, would you spit for the difference? The only guaranteed way to answer that question is to go back to the "quant jock" material of Chapter 4 and work out an example, so here goes. Let's not use the two extreme values, but instead, let's compare twenty-year results of investing $5,000 a year at 6% and at 8%.

$5,000 a year at 6% for 20 years = $183,928
$5,000 a year at 8% for 20 years = $228,810

That's about $45,000 and that's enough to buy a thirty-foot sailboat in good shape, a two-year-old Mercedes 560-SL, or 36,291 sixpacks of cheap beer. You make the choice, but *know for a fact* that it really does make a difference!

10

Investments You Don't Pay Any Tax On

What is the difference between a taxidermist and a tax collector? The taxidermist takes only your skin. MARK TWAIN

DISCLAIMER

The title of this chapter sounds like one of those "Send a check or call this toll-free number today—you absolutely can't lose on this deal" ads. And so we need to say a few words to keep things in perspective. True, we *are* going to talk here about certain investments whose returns (interest) are free of tax—but I wouldn't want you to get too excited. Sadly, the old aphorism "There just ain't any free lunch" still applies (my nearly-free lunches notwithstanding). By now, you have heard me say it so many times that you should be developing a Pavlovian response; you know, when you hear "tax-free," your knee jerks and you say "Let's see the fine print" or "Where's the down side?" If you get to the *last* response, I can trust you to protect yourself from the flocks of financial harpies out there. (If you still think there are free lunches, I haven't done a good enough job on you—so let me keep trying, okay?)

WHAT DOES TAX-EXEMPT MEAN?

As we first noted in Chapter 5, the interest you receive on *some* (we'll talk more about what "some" means in a minute) bonds issued by state and local governments is free of federal income tax. That's a fact! And there's more. The interest is also free of federal tax on some bonds sold by "authorities" (government-blessed folks who get together to do some things including building power dams, constructing low-income housing, constructing sewage lines, controlling pollution, building hospitals, and for all I know, saving snail darters, whales, and three-legged chickens).

Tax-exempt bonds are also free of state and local income tax in the state in which they are issued except for Illinois, Oklahoma, and Wisconsin. Better yet, if you live in Indiana or the District of Columbia, *all* tax-exempt municipal bond interest is exempt from state and local taxes regardless of where the bond was issued. Bonds issued in Puerto Rico are exempt from taxes in all states.

Why is this allowed, you may ask. Everybody else issues bonds on which the interest *is* taxable—why should some organizations get a better deal? The bottom line is that the federal government decided some time ago to make it easier for those state and local government organizations to borrow money (to do good things, of course)—and when they exempted the interest on these bonds from federal tax, they made it possible for these organizations to pay *less* interest. So if the Federation for the Arrangement of Regional Tree Counting Societies manages to get a ruling from the feds that it can issue tax-exempts, and if the current interest rate on *taxable* bonds is 10 percent, then the Federation for the Arrangement of Regional Tree Counting Societies (hereinafter referred to as FARTS) can probably promise to pay only 7 percent interest on their bonds. Look at what that saves them in interest! If they issue $1 million of bonds, instead of paying 10 percent or $100,000 a year interest, they can get by with, say, $70,000.

Now you're smart—and your first question is why would anybody buy a bond that yields 7 percent interest when the market rate is 10 percent. Good for you! The simple answer is that no one in her right mind *would* unless she figured that getting 7 percent tax exempt is as good as getting 10 percent taxable. Let's see if that's so.

If you're a single taxpayer, and if your taxable income ranges from something very near $17,850 to something very near $43,150, your tax rate is 28 percent as of this writing. So, go back to Chapter 5 to see what interest is worth when it's not taxed:

$$\text{Taxable equivalent yield} = \frac{\text{Tax exempt yield}}{1 - \text{your tax rate}}$$

(notice that we change the word *free* we used in Chapter 5 to "exempt"—that *proves* we are learning)

$$= \frac{7\%}{1 - .28}$$

$$= 9.72\%$$ (which is about half a gnat's eyebrow away from 10%)

So, being a public-spirited single citizen, you buy the FARTS bonds that yield 7 percent tax-exempt, and you earn almost a 10 percent taxable equivalent yield. In a word, you do well by doing good! The FARTS get their budget funded cheaper than they ever thought was possible; you get a nice interest income and are not penalized for doing good (and well), and everybody feels great.

BUT MY TAX RATE MAY BE MORE OR LESS THAN 28 PERCENT, COACH

True, true, and you can take your hand-held calculator and the formula we just used and make yourself a neat little table for lots of possible tax rates. But that would cut into your beer drinking time, so on page 162 it's done for most of the tax and investment rates that interest you—a free canapé if you please!

DOES THE TABLE COME WITH INSTRUCTIONS, COACH?

You bet it does! Let's do an example: The Northeast Regional Development System, a public organization (NERDS for short) advertises in your paper that they are offering tax-exempt bonds that pay 8 percent interest. On the same financial page, a private corporation, the Terrific Wholesaler of Ink, Towels, and Socks (TWITS for short) announces a *taxable* bond that pays 10 percent interest. What to do? Look in your table under 8 percent interest; come down that 8 percent column (columns go up and down; rows go left and right) till you hit your tax rate row—let's say yours is 28 percent. Read there the entry 11.1 percent. If you buy the NERDS tax-exempt bond, your taxable equivalent yield is 11.1%, but if you buy the TWITS taxable bond, your taxable

		If your tax-exempt bond pays this interest rate								
		5%	6%	7%	8%	9%	10%	11%	12%	
And if your tax rate is	15%	5.9%	7.1%	8.2%	9.4%	10.6%	11.8%	12.9%	14.1%	Then these are your taxable equivalent yields
	28%	6.9%	8.3%	9.7%	11.1%	12.5%	13.9%	15.3%	16.7%	
	33%	7.5%	9.0%	10.4%	11.9%	13.4%	14.9%	16.4%	17.9%	

equivalent yield is 10 percent. Unless you have an inherent bias for TWITS over NERDS, you ought to buy the tax-exempt bond. If you do that, you'll come out 1.1 percent better every year (11.1% − 10.0% = 1.1%).

ARE THOSE ALL THE INSTRUCTIONS THERE ARE?

Heavens, no—no choice is ever that simple, but that's how you begin. Lots of investors just won't buy securities issued by certain firms no matter what interest rate they offer. They just don't like their principles or causes. And many make it a practice to do good things for both public and private organizations, often suffering a reduction in investment yield to accomplish some private, social, or political goal. That may seem irrational on the face of it, but then that's the system of free choice we fight wars to preserve.

CAVEAT EMPTOR—INTO EACH LIFE A LITTLE RAIN MAY FALL

Then there is the little matter of risk. So far, we've scrupulously avoided comparing the risk between NERDS and TWITS. The TWITS have balance sheets and income statements that go back as far as they have been in business; they probably even have some financial projections five years into the future that they cooked up using their PC and some spreadsheet software. They can claim to show you that nothing short of nuclear war will prevent them from paying the interest on the bonds. The NERDS, on the other hand, have just organized and aren't nearly as certain about their future cash flows (out of which you hope to get your interest payment). They may not have nearly the financial sophistication of the TWITS, and without any operating history it may turn out—however sadly—that there is in fact very little demand for or support of their future activities. The bottom line is that even as a nonprofit public organization they could face financial ruin. If that happens, say bye-bye to the money you invested in their bonds. I'll say more about how this risk can often be reduced in a little while.

MATURITY MEANS MORE THAN GRAY HAIR

Suppose the TWITS agree to pay their bond back in five years, but the NERDS advertise their bond will not be paid back for fifteen years. If you aren't of a mindset to lock away your money for fifteen years, the TWITS look better. Of course, if you have a big pile of tax-exempt bonds in your investment portfolio, it may be okay to have some maturing every year or so for the next 15 years, but if you can afford to buy only one issue, things could get mighty dry during the next fifteen years.

But there are mitigating factors here too. There are markets every day in municipal tax-exempt bonds, and you can generally sell your bond any day you choose. But watch out. If you bought a 10 percent bond, and the interest rate on "tax exempts" (that's the uptown, high-class Wall Street generic word for them) has risen to 15 percent, you are in trouble. (So are the municipalities who have to pay that kind of interest!) All things considered, your $10,000 worth of 10 percent tax-exempt bonds is worth only about $6,667 today. How did we do that so fast? Algebra. Watch:

$$\text{Interest rate at issue} \times \text{face amount of bond} = \text{market interest rate today on bonds like this} \times \text{what the bond is worth today}$$

or in your case:

$$10\% \times \$10{,}000 = 15\% \times X \text{ (this is the unknown we are looking for)}$$

Putting it all together as we did in eighth grade algebra, we get:

$$X = \frac{10\% \times \$10{,}000}{15\%}$$

$$X = \$6{,}667$$

Even if you forgot all your algebra, you knew before we started this mathematical ordeal that you were in deep stuff, and it turns out your vibes were right. But all is not lost yet. If you wait until the bond matures, and if the issuing organization is financially able to pay you back, you *do* get $10,000. You just don't sell it at a "discount" for what the market says it's worth *today*. One final note here. It never really turns out quite like my algebra example—it comes *close* most of the time, but if the market rate *was* 15%, and if you looked in the *Wall Street Journal* today for a market quote on your bond, and if the paper said exactly $6,667, it would be a fluke—which if you are losing this much money on bonds ain't a bad fish to go after!

TELL ME MORE ABOUT TAX-EXEMPTS, COACH

Generally, tax exempts pay interest every six months, and they come with your name on them. That's called "registered," so if you put them under the mattress and someone rips off your mattress, or if you bury them in the yard and the dog makes off with them, no sweat.

Tax exempts generally come in units of $5,000 but there are exceptions to that rule. Ones that mature in a year often are sold only in blocks of $100,000, while some issuing organizations break down the issue into very small units (sometimes as low as $100) to make it easy for folks with very modest incomes to become a part of the deal.

ARE ALL BONDS ISSUED BY CITIES, COUNTIES, AND SUCH EXEMPT FROM FEDERAL TAXES?

Well, the answer used to be yes, but Congress changed all that with the 1986 tax law. They felt that tax-exempt bonds had gotten out of hand and that too much money raised by tax-

BONDAGE

exempts was being used for private projects, so they put the lid on so to speak. Now tax-exempts can't be used to finance things such as convention centers or sports coliseums owned by private organizations. And Congress set some new limits on the *amount* of tax-exempts that states could use for things such as multifamily housing projects. And in another blow, they eliminated the interest deduction that financial institutions got when they borrowed money to finance their purchase of tax-exempts. And finally, the feds limited the amount your town can issue to $50 per capita with a total ceiling of $150 million.

As a result of all these actions, the number of tax-exempt issues coming to the market will likely decline; and you know what that means—other things being equal, as they say, those people trying to buy these will bid up their prices, and consequently the interest yields are likely to fall. So it's like picking mushrooms: There's still lots of good stuff to eat, but you have to be more careful about what you are buying.

WHAT'S THE BAD WORD TO AVOID?

You know the phrase "The best laid plans often go astray." Well, the tax-exempt equivalent of that is "callable." Many tax-exempts have a call provision that permits the issuer to buy back the bonds at a specific time for a specified price. Now these times and these prices tend to work strictly in favor of the issuer, and against you and me! Say your hometown issues some tax-exempts at 10 percent interest, and five years later the market rate on such issues falls to 7 percent. If the appropriate legal language was put in, Hometown will likely "call" the issue—that is, pay it off—and issue new bonds at the current market rate of 7 percent. And where does that leave you and me? Sitting with our checking accounts full of money but with nowhere to invest that will yield us what we were getting. Always read the offering advertisement carefully and try to avoid tax-exempt issues with call provisions unless they promise reasonable reimbursement for being "called."

REDUCING SOME OF THE RISK

For about a dozen years, the proportion of tax-exempt bonds covered by private insurance has been increasing. Such insurance guarantees that the interest and principal will be paid on time. Of course, the insurance company that writes the policy could go broke too, but the few insurance companies that write these policies are pretty tough outfits. Before we leave this little blessing, please be aware that the insurance company only ensures (1) that you will get your interest, and (2) that *at maturity* you will get your money back. It does not ensure you if you have had a five-year bond for three years, and you need the money and interest rates have doubled, and you have to sell it for half of what you paid for it originally. That's your problem. And that's called market risk—you know the thing we explained with the risk-return graph. We'll show you another one of those ditties in just a second.

WHAT'S THE BOTTOM LINE, COACH? SHOULD I BUY SOME?

If you are in the 15 percent tax bracket, it doesn't pay you nearly as much to buy tax exempts as it does if you are in the 28 percent bracket. But even in the 15 percent tax bracket, you can sit down with your old friend:

$$\text{Taxable equivalent yield} = \frac{\text{Tax exempt yield}}{1-.15}$$

and get an answer, and compare that answer with the other stuff you are considering as investments. Then you'll be in shape to make up your mind. True, tax-exempts, strictly speaking, aren't quite as risk-free as the stuff we told you about in Chapter 10, but the difference isn't very much. On our risk-return graph, it looks something like this:

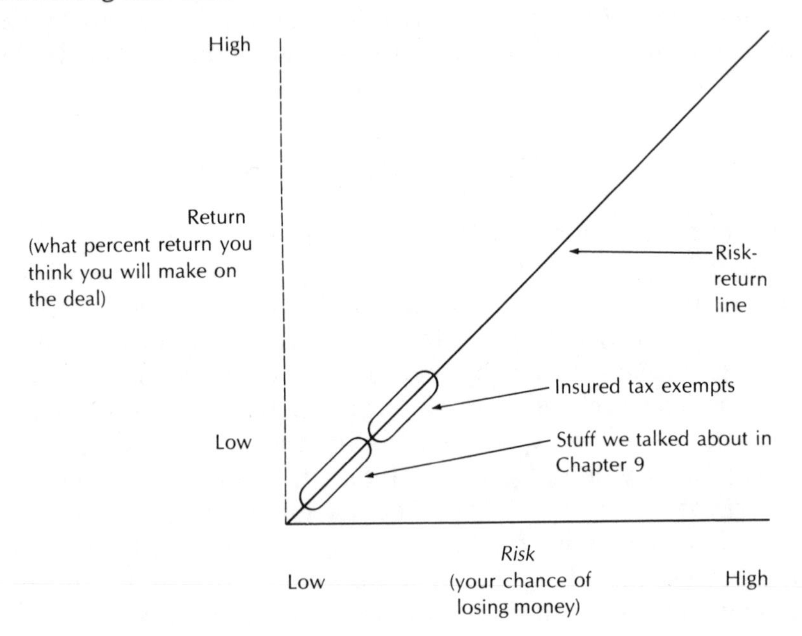

Figure 3

Conclusion: If the taxable equivalent returns on tax-exempts are *more* than 10 percent higher than you can get on the safe stuff from Chapter 9, do it. It works out this way: Say you can get 8 percent on the safe stuff from Chapter 9, and you are offered an insured tax exempt that fits all of your social, political, and maturity requirements whose taxable equivalent yield is 8.5 percent. Forget it; 8.5 percent is not 10 percent higher than 8 percent. If you are currently getting 7.5 percent on taxable safe stuff from Chapter 9 and you can buy a tax-exempt whose taxable equivalent yield is 8.75 percent, go on and buy it; 8.75 percent is more than 10 percent higher than 7.5 percent.

LAST PARAGRAPH

How do you buy tax-exempts? Easy, just talk to your broker (preferably a discount broker—they do the same thing at a much lower cost to you). If you are squeamish about putting all your financial eggs in one basket (that is, if tying up everything you want to invest in West Jonesburg Municipal Power bonds is not attractive to you), you can always buy shares in a mutual fund that owns *only* tax-exempt municipal bonds, and thus diversify your investment (which means get some eggs in each basket). More on the details of mutual funds in a later chapter. Bye!

Real Estate: The Kind You Can Reach Out and Touch

The best investment on earth is earth.
LOUIS GLICKMAN

MADE TO ORDER FOR YOU

Among the handful of investments that *really* make sense for the salaried person (particularly if you and your spouse combined are in the $20,000 to $70,000 income bracket), none is better suited for you than rental real estate. I speak here of the kind you can drive by and touch: the house next door, the duplex five blocks away, the house your folks used to live in, the condo you lived in before you bought your more expensive house, and, for that matter, any rentable property where the "numbers" (the stuff quant jocks and *you* now know how to do) make sense.

Okay, I realize you may never have owned a house (or condo) other than your own, and that you think of rental property as a big pain, and that your worst nightmare is being called at 3 A.M. by an irate tenant whose toilet is stopped up, and on and on and on. But just do me a favor. Read this chapter very carefully, work through the numbers with me, consider whether getting part of your withholding back every year or whether using other folks' money to create wealth for you are attractive thoughts, and let me answer what I think will be your questions. Then make up your mind about rental real estate as an investment.

WAR STORIES

There used to be a guy in High Point, North Carolina, named Charles Hughes who owned over 300 rental houses. He sold furniture and used to go around carrying pictures of each house in his coat pocket—sort of like grandparents carry photos of their grandchildren. He told a lot of folks that his biggest problem was spending the $30,000 he collected every month. He was probably right! As easy as you think it would be, getting rid of thirty grand a month (every month!) is probably harder than it seems. (But *some*body's got to do it.)

In my own case, my best friend Charlotte and I had been married about ten years when a friend of ours in the real estate business called me one day and asked if we could raise $2,000. The short answer was "no," but we had a bit of equity in our first house that Charlotte had built for $19,000 (house and lot) while I was overseas in the Air Force. We told our friend it was possible. We then signed new mortgage papers and notes somewhat ruefully, and gave our friend the money; he took our $2,000 and bought us a duplex. At the time, we were not sure what it was, what it was used for, and why we should be so foolish as to take title to one, but we went along, largely on faith and stupidity. As I recall, the duplex cost somewhere near $17,000, rented for $150 a month, had mortgage payments of about $85 a month, and took our entire home equity of $2,000 as the down payment.

Back then, we were not sure this was a smart thing to do with our home equity. Now as we look back, it was the single smartest investment we have made in our lives! We kept buying duplexes and houses and other real estate since that first one, and though we are far, far from the 300 rental houses the man in High Point owned, we have done well with this strategy. We *still* own that first duplex that we bought for about $17,000. Today, it's worth conservatively $75,000 and rents for about $700 a month. It's been mortgaged, remortgaged, painted, rescreened, reporched, air conditioned, reroofed, rewired, replumbed, and rerented twenty times. In the twenty-eight years we've owned it, it has done a lot of things for us including:

1. Allowed us to get withholding back from the feds legally
2. Provided us with cash to spend
3. Permitted us to remortgage it and buy more rental property with the money we got from doing this

4. Enabled us to own something that has increased greatly in value (investment mavens call that "appreciation")
5. Caused us sleepless nights early on when one side was vacant for a month and we didn't know whether we could make the mortgage payment
6. Brought us near heart failure the first time the rental agent called and said that the roof was leaking and would have to be replaced, and
7. Given us a good bit of self-confidence to make other, non-real estate investments

In this chapter, I'm going to lead you by the hand, step by step, through the process of evaluating, acquiring, owning, renting, and benefitting from rental real estate. I'm going to show you how you can do what Charlotte and I have done (on a scale that you believe makes sense to *you*). And I'm going to demonstrate why *even under the new tax laws,* owning rental real estate may be the best thing you can get going for yourself if wealth creation is really what you want to do. It will take some quant jock work; some new terms will need to be defined; and we will need to work through a bunch of examples together; but when we're done, you will understand the process and you will be able to do it yourself. So let's go.

ANOTHER OF THOSE RIDICULOUS GRAPHS

Before we start the lesson, you need to consider once again the relationship of risk and return in this type of investment. Now don't get scared—I'm not going to tout you into land speculation, limited partnerships in sanitary landfills, or development of remote tropical islands. No, we're going to examine *very carefully* how you can benefit from investing in rental real estate, the kind Charlotte and I have. And what's the risk in doing this? In my judgment, rental real estate for folks like you belongs on our risk-return graph right where I've got it shown below:

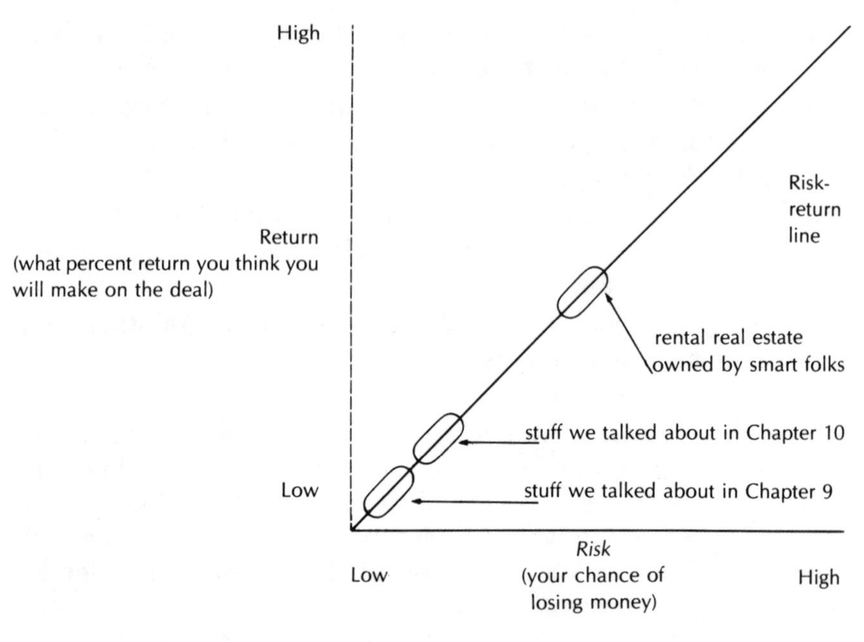

Figure 4

LEXICON

Remember the first time you studied a new subject—anything from accounting to zoology, from civics to strength of materials, or from biology to rug weaving. The first thing you had to do was *learn new terms*—a new language, if you please. This is no different, and we need to take a short side trip so you can master the language of real estate. Look at it this way. If you are going to dig way down in your piggy bank and raise some cash or mortgage your home to raise cash, or whatever it takes to raise some cash, and then if you (and your spouse or significant other) are going to sign a bunch of legal papers that obligate you to do some things for a number of years, you need to understand what in the hell you are getting into. And that's what we'll start with right now. If it's too elementary for you, just read faster and quit complaining.

1. *Appreciation:* the difference between what you pay for a piece of property and what you sell it for. Unfortunately this can be either a positive number (that's what we plan for it to be) or a negative number (which either means you have really screwed things up or your local economy has run on the rocks). Appreciation in rental property is *not* what it was fifteen years ago, but if you are a careful, smart, patient shopper, it is still there for you.
2. *Leverage:* This word describes the relationship between the down payment you make on the property and what you pay for it. Leverage can be anything between 0% (you pay all cash for a property) and 100% (you finance the entire purchase price). In the case of the first duplex Charlotte and I bought, we made a $2,000 down payment on a $17,000 duplex, so we leveraged $15,000/$17,000 or 88% of the price. You can still do that today! *Too little* leverage and you have too much of your own money invested to make a decent return on it. *Too much* leverage and you've borrowed so much money that you may have a problem making the mortgage payments. With the right percentage leverage, you have enough of someone else's money working for you and you make a better return. Just like everything else in life, including Goldilocks and the three bears, truth is always somewhere between the extremes.
3. *Depreciation:* An accounting term that describes how much you claim to the feds on your tax return that your duplex is losing in value every year. (In theory, buildings lose value as they age owing to physical deterioration and obsolescence.) Mephistophelian in origin, quite complex, and often misunderstood even by MBA students, depreciation is *very* important to us. Suppose you buy a rental house for $53,000 and you look in the tax law to see "how fast you can write it off" (that is, how *much* depreciation you can claim a year—so you can persuade the IRS you are losing money—so you'll get some of your withholding back). You'll find the answer to be 27½ years. Next step: Subtract a little bit for the land value, because only the house can be depreciated. (Houses rot, blow down, or get eaten by termites; land sup-

posedly lasts forever—at least in the tax code.) So we take off $3,000 for land and assign $50,000 to the house itself. Watch now, you divide your house value by 27.5 years to get your annual depreciation:

$$\frac{\$50{,}000}{27.5} = \$1818$$

Now what do we have? On your tax return, you claim a $1,818 expense for depreciation, even though you know that your duplex will probably be worth *more* every year that you own it. Why more? Because inflation in property values (a rising cost of living, building, dying, and sex) affects the value of your duplex, too. I'm assuming two things here: (1)

A MAN'S RENTAL PROPERTY IS HIS CASTLE

you live in a part of the country with a reasonably healthy economy, and (2) you'll be careful enough not to grossly overpay on that first duplex you buy. Now the funny thing about depreciation expense that you need to reflect on, understand, and *remember* is you don't actually write anyone a check for the $1,818 but you get to claim it as an expense. So no *cash* goes anywhere but you get to subtract dollars regardless. That fact makes it very important to folks trying to get some of their withholding back!

4. *Operating Expenses:* This simple notion includes just about everything you spend to keep your duplex going *except* depreciation. It includes: property taxes, repairs, interest on your mortgage (only interest on what you borrowed, not the repayment of the money—i.e., principal you borrowed), getting rid of bugs, insurance, and paying your kids $20 a week to cut the grass (yes, you *can* do that and shift income to your kids, but much more on ways to do that in a later chapter).
5. *Equity Buildup:* Each year, if you pay off some of the mortgage you owe on your duplex, and if prices of real estate keep rising (which they will wherever local economies are in decent shape) your *equity* (the difference between what it's worth and what you owe on it) will increase. The amount by which your equity increases is called "equity build-up." It's one measure of how well you're doing with the duplex.
6. *Cash Flow:* When you think about it, this is a very simple notion, but one that plagues even folks who have studied accounting. It goes something like this: If you write down on one piece of paper all of the rent you take in from your duplex this year, and if you write down on another piece of paper everything you paid cash or wrote a check for this year (that means everything except depreciation), the difference is your cash flow. If your cash flow stays positive, things generally turn out fairly well; if it gets a little bit negative, and you are employed, you can make up the difference every month out of your salary; if it gets real negative, bad things start to happen. First, the mortgage holder generally

gets mad and shortly thereafter the sheriff turns up with some papers and takes your duplex. See why looking at cash flow is important?

7. *Tax-deductible Loss:* This is what you tell the I.R.S. you lost on the duplex every year. (Yes, lost, even though your cash flow was positive.) Go get two new pieces of paper. On one, write down all of the rent you took in this year; on the other, write down everything for which you wrote a check. When you get to your mortgage payment, although it's one check, it has two parts. Write down mortgage *interest;* that's tax deductible. Do *not* write down the mortgage *principal,* because that isn't really an expense, only giving the guy back what he lent you. Then you also write down, as an expense, depreciation. (Remember that depreciation is *not* a cash expense item but a presumed loss in value that the I.R.S. lets you subtract.) The difference between what you have on the first piece of paper and what you have on the second piece (income minus expenses) is your "tax-deductible loss." The bigger it is, the more withholding you get back. This is what they mean when they say "tax shelter"—that is, something that shelters your income from taxes. Of course, if you have a big tax deductible loss and you also have a big negative cash flow, those bad things (including the sheriff) that we talked about before can start to happen again. *The trick is to keep the cash flow at just about zero, but max out on the tax deductible loss*—that is, get yourself the biggest tax shelter you can and shelter as much of your income from income taxes as possible. If I've thoroughly confused you, it's probably late in the day, so have a beer and be patient. I'll show you examples of all of this in a jiffy.
8. *Taxable Profit:* Here we go again. Say you have very low operating expenses and high rents on your duplex, and you have had it for 27.5 years so the I.R.S. won't let you claim any more depreciation. That means the income on the first piece of paper is high and the expenses on the second piece of paper are very low; thus, you will show a taxable profit on the duplex and have to pay some tax. Since (at this writing) the most you'll get socked with is 28 percent, take your

72 percent, stop complaining, and be happy you live in a free country that lets you do all these evil things to your own government.

It might be helpful right here if you went back to pages 81–87 in Chapter 5 and reread the tax-related definitions there. Life and definitions are never quite as simple as I make them out to be, but this is not the time or place to go into every nuance of real estate accounting and real estate tax law. What I've shown you here is enough for you to get a good gut feeling for the fundamentals of rental real estate. Don't try it unless you *do* understand what's here. But also don't be reluctant to ask your friendly CPA to go over it with you again (and again maybe)—that's smart! If he doesn't have the patience to help you understand it, hire yourself one who does!

HOW DO YOU MAKE MONEY FROM RENTAL REAL ESTATE?

There are only three ways you benefit when you buy a property to rent, and here they are:

1. When you have written checks for all your bills, whatever rent income you have left over at the end of the year is your *net cash flow.* That's one way you win in this game—you have cash left over.
2. When you cipher up your income tax return, you either show that the duplex made a profit or sustained a loss. If you show a loss, you get to deduct that loss from your other income (salary, dividends, interest), which reduces your tax bill.
3. Unless you were blind drunk when you bought it, it's reasonable to expect the value of the property to increase at about the same rate as the cost of living. Some years more, some years less, but building houses and duplexes isn't getting any cheaper, and the value of yours will reflect that fact in the years to come. If the city puts up a sanitary landfill in

your yard, you lose. If they put up a new civic center, you win—the Lord giveth and the Lord taketh away. Of course, when you sell the property, you pay income tax *on* this gain in value but our tax laws are generous compared to those in other countries, and you get to keep most of what you make.

Which of these benefits is most important? This is a very difficult question to answer, but it's a good one! If you make a large down payment (usually an error), your mortgage payments will be very small and you will generate a whole lot of cash. If you pay taxes at the highest rate, tax deductible losses will be more valuable to you; thus, the tax shelter value of the property may become more important. And if the city does build a new civic center in your yard, the rise in value of your property will likely eclipse the other two benefits completely.

In sum, the question doesn't have one answer. You get out your pencil and calculator (as we'll show in a minute) and you push some numbers, and then you see what things are likely to look like in the future. Only then can you see if and how wealth is likely to be created for you.

DIDN'T I READ SOMEWHERE HERE THAT THE NEW TAX LAW KILLED REAL ESTATE AS AN INVESTMENT?

If you did, then you weren't reading carefully. The new tax law in 1986 may have killed rental real estate as a good investment for high-income individuals and syndicates, but it specifically saved it for *you*! As a matter of fact, it is one of the few tax shelters (there's that nice word again) left to you under the new tax law.

Let's look at the specific language of the 1986 tax law. Up to $25,000 a year of tax losses from rental properties can be used to offset your other income (stuff like salary, interest and dividends) *as long as* your adjusted gross income (that's the line that counts on your Form 1040) is under $100,000. And that should take care of just about everyone who reads this book! There you have it—a real big bonus from the I.R.S. for people with smaller adjusted gross incomes. This means that you can do things with real estate that generate tax-deductible losses up to $25,000, and use those to shelter your other income from taxes and get some of your withholding back. It works like this:

Penelope Smith

Adjusted gross income from salary and dividends	$41,300
Tax deductible losses from her rental real estate this year	7,500
Revised adjusted gross income	33,800
Tax at 28%	9,464
Total tax withheld this year	11,564
Refund due ($11,564–9464)	2,100

Let's put it another way. If Penelope Smith pays 28 percent federal taxes, then every single dollar of real estate-generated loss that she comes up with is worth 28 cents to her in taxes saved. Things are looking better and better.

For you to become eligible for this deal, in addition to having an adjusted gross income of less than $100,000 (the easy part for most of us) you have to "actively participate" in the management of the property. This does *not* mean that you have to get up at 3 A.M. and unstop a john, or that you even have to go around every month cornering tenants and collecting the rent money. No, but you *must* make the management decisions involved in your duplex(es), such as deciding what rents to charge, approving new tenants, approving major repair expenditures, and approving the purchase of new equipment (a furnace, for example). You can still have someone else, including a professional property manager, take care of the johns, the repairs, and the collecting of rents, but you have to make the big decisions—a fairly easy thing to arrange.

And if you can't quite get up all the bread it would take to buy that nice twelve-unit apartment house on the next street, you can get together a partnership of some of your relatives or friends (friends are generally better) and buy it as a group. As long as you own at least 10 percent of the partnership, you can still claim your share of the tax-deductible loss it generates.

NUMBERS—SHOW US SOME NUMBERS

Say you find this nice little house a mile from where you live that's for sale by the owner for $80,000. Since there's no real estate commission involved in this sale, you can probably buy it for somewhat less. Say you really believe that you can get it for $75,000 with a 10 percent down payment. Say also that the owner will take a twenty-five-year mortgage back for the balance at 8¾ percent interest. Your best estimate of rent is $810 a month; insurance will cost $410 annually, and local property taxes are $740 a year. Should you run out and buy it now?

Absolutely not. A thousand times no. *Never* make an investment without pushing some numbers first. Once you sign the note and deed, the deal is done and if you made a mistake or forgot to include something, or paid too much, you are locked in, often for years. Real estate isn't like a used car—you can sell a car with a newspaper ad in a week at the right price. A house (or a duplex) is much more difficult to sell, so be a quant jock instead of an impetuous purchaser and get your numbers together first and push them hard—paper and pencils are cheap.

WATCH OUT: QUANT JOCK IN ACTION

Let's make our best guess as to what will happen during the first year that you own the property. A little later, we can extend that for additional years, but if you are comfortable doing it for the first year, you can do it for fifty years! The following table makes sense for estimating what's likely to happen in the first year you own the house. There is nothing sacred (or particularly innovative) about this format—you should use one that makes you comfortable, and you can add anything that helps you better grasp what you will get into if you buy the house. So tell the owner that you'll get back to her in a day or two (and let her stew a little about whether you will be back) while we get to work:

Rental income: 12 mos. × $810		$9,720
Operating expenses:		
Property taxes	$740	
Repairs (it's hard to get by with less than 2 percent of the value, even if nothing's broken; in later years, this is too little, but we'll adjust it later)	1,500	
Insurance	410	
Pest control (six times annually)	90	
Interest on mortgage (8¾% × $67,500 financed) the first year; the IRS lets you deduct this (but not the principal)	5,906	
Yard maintenance (great thing for your teenage kid to do to earn income that will be taxed at a lower percentage)	240	
Total estimated operating expenses		$8,886
Depreciation:		
Purchase price	$75,000	
Less something for the value of the land; the feds won't let you depreciate land because strictly speaking it never "wears out"; we can probably get by with something near $5,000	− 5,000	
Amount to be depreciated	$70,000	
Divided by 27.5 years	$2,545 a year depreciation	
Mortgage payment		
Twenty-five year, 8¾ percent loan on $67,500	$554.97/month or $6,660/year	

CASH IN, CASH OUT—WILL IT BE POSITIVE?

Now that we have everything we need to do our number work on one page in a reasonable format, let's begin our attack. First, let's see what the *cash-flow situation* looks like. If you're a bit rusty on cash flow:

Cash-flow projection:

Rental income coming in		$9,720
Cash going out (everything you wrote a check for this year):		
Operating expenses *except* for mortgage interest	$2,980	
Mortgage payment (principal *and* interest)	6,660	
No depreciation (remember, we don't write a check for this)	0	
Total cash going out		$9,640
Net cash flow		$ 80

So far so good—we have a positive cash flow, and if everything works out as planned, we won't have to dip into our salary income to support the house.

NOW FOR THE TAX SHELTER PART

This time we want to figure what we'll lose for tax purposes, so here we go:

Tax shelter projection

Rental income coming in		$9,720
Operating expenses (including mortgage interest)	$8,886	
Depreciation	2,545	
Total deductible expenses		$11,431
Tax deductible loss ($9720 – $11,431)		$1,711

AND NOW FOR THE APPRECIATION PART

If we bought the house at the market price and we expect housing to rise about as fast as the cost of living index, we are looking at something near a 4 percent increase in value per year. Of course, this is never guaranteed, but look at what has happened to the value of your house in the last ten years! Four percent is actually a modest (sort of "bearish," to use the Wall Street term) estimate of value increase, but better to be bearish and come out smiling ten years from now than the other way around. So, 4 percent of $75,000 is an estimated appreciation in value of $3,000 a year. Not bad for a bear!

PUTTING IT ALL TOGETHER, WHAT WOULD WE GET IF WE BOUGHT THE HOUSE?

What good did we do with the $7,500 we used as a down payment for the house? First, we just about broke even on the cash flow. We didn't have to put any more money in the deal, and we had a few bucks left over at the end of the year but hardly enough to count. Second, we generated a tax shelter of $1,711. Since we're probably paying 28 percent tax, that $1,711 is worth 28% × $1,711, or $479. If the feds have been withholding enough out of our salary to pay all of our federal tax, we'll get $479 of that withholding back if we buy this house. Finally, our $7,500 down payment got us in a deal that, conservatively figuring, will be worth $3,000 more every year.

Let's count all that up at the same time:

Net cash flow ($9,720 – $9,640)	$ 80
Value to us of getting our withholding back (28% × $1,711)	479
Projected appreciation (let's go ahead and deduct the income tax on 28 percent we'll have to pay if we sell the house later)	
$3,000 × 72% (net to us)	2,160
Total good we did with our $7,500	$2,719

Now since we've already figured in the tax on the appreciation, and since the value of getting our withholding back is also an after-tax return, and since the house loses money we don't owe any money on the $80 cash, *everything* here, yes, the whole darn

$2,719, is an after-tax return. It turns out to be an after-tax return of:

$$\frac{\$2{,}719}{\$7{,}500} \times 100\% = 36.3\%$$

which is higher than anything we've talked about so far. As a matter of fact, it's higher than anything we'll talk about from here to the end of the book, too! See why rental real estate, carefully bought, conservatively estimated, and well managed can be a good deal for folks with your income? Quick, call the lady who owns the house, but sound as cool as you can. Ask her to give you a 30 year mortgage with only $6,000 down, and watch what happens to your after-tax return if she says yes. Call the termite inspector too before you sign anything!

THIRTY-SIX PERCENT COMPARED TO WHAT?

I had a professor in college who always answered questions with "Let's examine the alternatives." So let's. Had we decided *not* to buy the house, and had we invested our $7,500 down payment in the best-yielding U.S. Government security available to us (in today's interest rate market that's a yield of about 8.7 percent on a 30-year bond), our total "take" before tax would be 8.7 percent × $7,500, or $652.50 a year. This is, of course, taxable, and after we paid the 28 percent federal tax, we'd have $469.80 left, for an after-tax return of 6.26 percent, about a sixth of what the house can return. Of course, the risk in buying a house is higher than the risk in buying a government bond (I showed you that already), but is it six times as high? No way! What about the *maturity* problem we talked about in Chapter 9? To get 8.7 percent on a safe bond, we'll have to wait thirty years. If interest rates rise in the meantime and we need to sell the bond, we'll take a bath on it. Of course, if we have to sell the house next year, the real estate market may be down and we'll lose something there too. Sounds like about a draw on maturity. Comes out in my judgment and experience that salaried folks who don't mind a bit of work, some hassles now and then, an occasional busted water pipe, and a hole in the roof once in a while ought to think seriously about rental real estate for part of their investable capital.

BUT I DON'T WANT A PHONE CALL IN THE MIDDLE OF THE NIGHT

Oh yes, the stopped-up-toilet-at-3-A.M. phone call. I was wondering when you'd ask about that. I mentioned professional property management earlier, but you shrewdly noted no expense item for that in my calculations. Many owners of rental houses manage them themselves and save the fee—particularly when they own only one house, or maybe two. Property managers charge a percentage of the rent; in my area, it's 6 to 8 percent, depending on the agent. To find a property manager, look in the yellow pages or ask a real estate broker about them. Some real estate brokerage firms offer this service. If you hire a property manager, it will put a big dent in cash flow but will also add to the deductible expenses of your rental property. Push the numbers before you decide, and be honest with yourself about what you're willing to do in the way of selecting tenants and calling repair people.

SUPPOSE I HAVE AN AVERSION TO OWING MONEY, COACH; WHAT THEN?

It's not written in stone somewhere that you have to mortgage a rental property. In fairness, however, I point out that Americans owed about $1.5 trillion in mortgages in 1985. You *can* take the money that your dear old Uncle Alphonse left you last year and pay cash for the whole thing! In fact, if you do that, the owner may even give you a bit better deal on the price. Let's go through our numbers very quickly assuming that you have decided to pay $75,000 cash for the house we just examined. How good an investment would it be now?

To begin with, the rental income would be the same; so would property taxes, repairs, insurance, pest control, and yard maintenance. Depreciation wouldn't change either. In fact, the only change is that there would be no deduction for mortgage interest and repayment of principal. Here's how the numbers look now:

Cash-flow projection:		
Rental income coming in		$9,720
Cash going out		
Operating expenses		−2,980
Net cash flow a year		$6,740
Tax shelter projection:		
Rental income coming in		$9,720
Operating expenses	$2,980	
Depreciation	$2,545	
Total deductible expenses		−5,525
Oops! Now we have *taxable income* because without the mortgage interest to pay, we actually *make* money on the house.		$4,195
Appreciation projection:		
Same as before, $3,000 a year		

So, let's count up all three benefits and see what the total is:

Net cash flow is now	$6,740
The house has *no* tax shelter value; in fact it makes money, so we'll owe tax on the $4,195 profit of 28 percent, or $1,175. This obviously is a cost, not a benefit.	−1,175
And the appreciation is the same as before ($3,000 × 72% net to us)	2,160
Total good we did under this option with our $75,000	$7,725

That's a lot more good than we did when we financed 90 percent of the purchase price. But *whoa*! You also have a lot more invested—$75,000 to be exact. So the after-tax return comes out to be:

$$\frac{\$7{,}725}{\$75{,}000} \times 100\% = 10.3\%$$

This isn't nearly the 36.3 percent that we earned when we put down only 10 percent of the purchase price. Right! And that's what leverage (the neat idea we introduced on page 177 of this chapter) is all about. When you use other people's money and just a bit of your own, your part earns much higher returns. As I agreed earlier in Chapter 6, owing money is only evil when:

1. You never *intend* to pay it back.
2. You have no idea *how* to pay it back.
3. You owe it to a brother-in-law you despise.

LET'S THINK LONG TERM FOR A MINUTE

Life as the owner of a rental property doesn't start and end in the first year; it goes on and on, unless of course the city builds a civic center next door and some developer walks up and offers you half a million for the lot! In that case, say yes and sign whatever he puts in front of you. Otherwise, you need to be interested in and aware of what happens after the first year. On pages 192–93, I've shown a tabular presentation to help you think through the next five years in a systematic and comfortable way.

Notice that our projections are conservative—that's the best way to make them in the real estate rental business. Rents are projected to rise only 5 percent a year—they will probably do better than this. Repairs are projected to rise 10 percent a year—they probably won't rise that fast. Most other expenses are projected to rise about even with a rising cost of living, which they have done historically. All in all, we have made a fairly conservative projection of the next five years.

What does it show then? First, notice that our *cash flow* rises. This is due primarily to rising rental income, tempered of course by rising expenses too. Next, watch what happens to our tax shelter. It falls each year. This is primarily because depreciation stays constant (under the current tax law) while rental

Five-year Projection for Rental House

No.	Item	Assumptions (*your* best informed guess)	Year 1 from page 185	Year 2	Year 3	Year 4	Year 5
1.	Rental income	Will probably increase at about 5 percent a year (pretty conservative)	$9,720	$10,206	$10,716	$11,252	$11,815
2.	Property tax	Tends to go up at about 5 percent a year	740	777	816	857	899
3.	Repairs	Probably will rise at 10 percent a year (more than adequate)	1,500	1,650	1,815	1,997	2,197
4.	Insurance	Rose very rapidly from 1984–1988; will tend to rise more slowly, say 3 percent a year	410	422	435	448	461
5.	Pest control	Rises with cost of living, say 5 percent a year	90	95	100	105	110
6.	Mortgage interest	Falls as you pay off the mortgage—but *very, very* slowly	5,906	5,840	5,769	5,691	5,606

7.	Yard maintenance	Probably will rise at 5 percent a year	240	252	265	278	292
8.	Depreciation	Fixed unless you want to do time in federal prison (or the tax law changes again, and it could!)	2,545	2,545	2,545	2,545	2,545
9.	Mortgage payment	Stays fixed as long as you have a fixed rate instead of a variable rate mortgage.	6,660	6,660	6,660	6,660	6,660
	Cash flow projection (cash in − cash out) just as we did on page 186; or no. 1 − 2 − 3 − 4 − 5 − 7 −9		$80	$350	$625	$907	$1,196
	Tax shelter projection (rental income minus operating expenses minus depreciation just as on page 186; or no. 1 − 2 − 3 − 4 − 5 − 6 − 7 − 8		−1,711	−1,375	−1,029	− 669	− 295
	Appreciation (4 percent a year, each time on the new value)		3,000	3,120	3,245	3,375	3,510
	TOTAL GOOD WE ARE DOING WITH OUR $7,500 Cash flow + (tax shelter × 0.28) + (appreciation × 0.72), just as we did on page 187		$2,719	$2,981	$3,250	$3,524	$3,806

income rises, thereby reducing our loss each year. Finally, notice that the appreciation benefit rises by 4 percent each year over the previous year's value. The net of all this is that the "total good we are doing with our $7,500 investment" rises each year. I have computed the *percent* increases to be:

Year 1 to year 2	9.7%
Year 2 to year 3	9.0%
Year 3 to year 4	8.4%
Year 4 to year 5	8.0%

Two final notes before you sell the family jewels and buy three houses like this. First, your $7,500 investment in the house increases a lot each year because you are (1) paying off the mortgage, and (2) the value of the house increases, which increases what we defined earlier as "equity build up." If you do another two minutes of quant-jock stuff, you'll actually see that by the fifth year you have about $27,184 equity in your house (on paper). If that scares you, just remember that we've assumed that the value of the house will rise by 4 percent a year ($16,250 over five years from the table on page 193) to a total value of $91,250, while the mortgage balance will decline by over $3,000 (from $67,500 down to $64,066) because you have been diligent in making your mortgage payments. Put all of this together and your equity will be about $27,184 in five years. Compare that with the total good you are doing in the fifth year from the table and you get:

$$\frac{\$3{,}806}{\$27{,}184} \times 100\% = 14.0\% \text{ after tax return}$$

That's not the 36.1 percent you were making after-tax in the first year because your house is worth more, thus you have *more* invested. Why are we arguing? The 14.0% after-tax is better than almost anything else that fits the wealth-creation needs of salaried folks like you! And one quick word about the major component of that equity buildup—appreciation: You never know exactly what this figure is until you sell your house. Here, we've *assumed* 4 percent annually. You should try to dig up the correct average rate of increase for your local market (try the newspaper or a realtor) and then adjust it for the future based on your judgment of local conditions. Remember, you're trying to project what will happen for, say, five or ten years—long enough to smooth out the effects of the typical business cycle, or else as long as you care to look ahead.

No I *didn't* forget the second note. I have a friend who is a utility contractor. You know, someone who digs holes in the ground to bury water pipes, electric lines, and sewer lines. What really kills his day is when his back hoe hits rock—then he has to stop digging and do a lot of different things (dynamite, pray, curse, borrow money, and hope). Some of these things are very, very expensive. So, he puts a "rock allowance" in each bid where his survey suggests that he may hit rock. In the rental real estate business, you need to have a rock allowance too. You can also call it "contingency." It covers roofs; worn-out refrigerators, stoves, and air conditioners; unexpected street assessments; longer than normal vacancies; and rent price wars. Now, let's go back to the beginning. My best friend (and main squeeze) Charlotte Levin and I have owned rental property (houses, duplexes, and apartment buildings) for over twenty-five years. I cipher up our average after-tax return at about 21 percent. It ain't 36.1, but it ain't too shabby either.

DICK'S TEN-POINT CHECKLIST FOR PROSPECTIVE LANDLORDS

1. Buy property in your town—it's difficult to manage property a thousand miles away, and, besides, it gives you a great sense of accomplishment to drive by once in a while and look at it. It also angers you if you see that the tenant has busted out the screens.
2. Never get emotionally involved with either a piece of property or a tenant. Rental property is not your home; it is an investment, and you do not decorate it as though *you* lived there. Tenants are generally nice folks, but their responsibility is to look after your property and pay the rent on time. Don't let them weasel out of either responsibility.

3. Try to buy from owners, not through brokers. You save the sales commission and often can do better on the price. Don't be afraid to negotiate with the owner for a better price or better terms on the mortgage. If negotiating bothers you, either get someone to do it for you or stay out of the rental business. (You *can* invest in real estate in impersonal trusts called REITs that are traded on the New York Stock Exchange. But you don't get the tax shelter, and it's a different kind of deal altogether.)
4. Don't pay more than 120 times the monthly rental of a piece of property. That is a rough (very rough) rule of thumb, which, if you do about four hours of number crunching, you can satisfy yourself that it works most of the time.
5. Make as low a down payment as you can and still manage to keep the cash-flow situation where you can handle it. This does wonders for your investment return, especially for people with modest sums to invest.
6. Don't ever buy a cheap piece of property in the wrong location. Moving a house or duplex is vexing to do and rarely makes money. Location need not be high class, but unless you have designs on being a slum landlord, don't buy in the slums. The first thing that happens is you get your picture in the local paper.
7. Do projections. Do them two or three times. Get someone to check them. Be conservative, be honest, be diligent in collecting figures, but *never* buy a piece of property until you have "run the numbers." Do not succumb to pressure that a seller may exert on you to make a deal before you have time to check it to your satisfaction. If necessary, just walk away.
8. Don't speculate on raw land. I'll say that again: Don't try to make a million speculating on raw land. Experts sometimes lose their shirts doing this, and it can tie up money for years.
9. Hire your children to do whatever maintenance they can do: painting, yard work, cleaning, fixing, simple carpentry, stuff like that. Pay them for it and make them declare the income for tax purposes. They will pay only about half the tax you

will on whatever you pay them, which is a good income-tax shifting tactic to learn. More on this later.

10. It's difficult to make any money renting high-priced property. That's a fact. Tenants who pay rents of $1,000 or more per month want their lawn and yard manicured, their home painted annually, their appliances of the finest quality, the house full of extras such as jacuzzis, and instant repair service. All these extras will eventually bankrupt you. A good rule to follow is never buy a rental property that is as nice as the one you live in now. Not too egalitarian perhaps, but a good rule to follow.

COLD SHOWER

Well, you know by now that I'm very high on real estate. Our investments in rental property have been very kind to Charlotte and me, and I am grateful. I am also prejudiced. But let me add that I have had the great good fortune to live in a town with steady growth, high employment, and no wrenching boom-or-bust cycles. Furthermore, and equally to the point, I have an affinity for investing in tangible things—investments you can drive by and see, such as bricks and mortar. You may recall that I've used that term before—*affinity*—and think it worth mentioning again. Affinities matter. Some people—you may be one—have absolutely no "feel" for real estate, but understand and *like* stocks and bonds. Then there was that graduate student of mine who consistently made money on photographs (against any sane advice) because she had an affinity for them. So by all means follow *your* affinities, but when you do, for heaven's sake remember to diversify your investments too—spread your money around in different and relatively safe things such as we've talked about in previous chapters.

Now, who should *not* invest in real estate? I would say people who should not invest include those who

- Have absolutely no affinity for it
- Live in a part of the country with a longtime depressed econ-

omy and whose expected remaining lifetime is shorter than the region's expected recovery time (come to think of it, maybe they should move)

- Hate to negotiate
- Need a high level of liquid assets (or portable ones such as diamonds) all of the time
- Have a consistent preference for very low risk—that is, a position farther down and to the left on our risk-return line
- Never stay longer than a year in one place
- Don't fancy material encumbrances (same thing, really, as "feel no affinity for")

And that's the crop, I do believe. Still leaves a lot of people who can build a lot of wealth very nicely given reasonable effort and interest. And you?

12

Owning a Piece of a Company, a Piece of a Company's Debt, or a Piece of a Piece of Something

It is speculation when you lose; investment when you win. Reflections of a Batchelor

COMING ATTRACTIONS, SOME MAYBE NOT SUITABLE FOR YOU

This chapter introduces and comments on four kinds of investments that you should understand even if you decide not to try any of them:

- *Common Stocks:* A share of common stock is nothing more than a piece of the ownership of a company (a piece of the equity if you like); if you add together all of the common stockholders in a corporation, they own it.
- *Corporate Bonds:* A corporate bond (much like the government bonds, notes, and bills we talked about in Chapter 9) is a legal paper in which the company promises to pay you a certain rate of interest (usually fixed) on money you *lend* the company.
- *Preferred Stocks:* A misnomer, since this kind of investment is really not preferred over anything (except maybe air). Preferred stock is also evidence that you own part of a corporation, but in this case the corporation has promised to do some things for its preferred stockholders that it doesn't do for its common stockholders. This can be both bad and good, as we shall see.
- *Mutual Funds:* A mutual fund is a collection of stocks (or other securities) put together by a company (which believes these will appreciate in value or pay out good income for both); this company then sells shares in itself to folks like you and me. Mutual funds can also be collections of lots of other things as we shall see shortly.

If you go back and read the language of the first sentence in this chapter, you'll see that I said "that you should understand." That is a lot different from saying "that you should buy." It's as different as night and day, as black and white, or as my piano playing and Errol Garner's! I have never been a big advocate of stocks and bonds (the private, not the government kind) for folks like you who want to create wealth on a modest salary. And I'll tell you why in detail shortly. But *you* are the person who must take the choice. You will decide whether you have an affinity for these investments (as opposed, say, to the sticks and bricks of a rental house), and so we'll spend some time together examining these investments, noting how they have behaved, being sure we understand fully the risks involved in each of them, and becoming more familiar with what they are and what they can do. However, as the advertisements say, "This does not represent in any way an endorsement of this product by the management!"

COMMON STOCKS (OWNING A PIECE OF AMERICA)

When you buy a common stock, you buy a piece of a corporation. The seventh-grade civics books claim that you (the stockholders) control the corporation, say what it will do, who runs it, and even what color its stock certificates will be. But small stockholders (a single share or a few shares) actually have little or nothing to say about any of this. It's like everything else in life—the big owners get to make the decisions in a corporation; the rest of us get one copy of the annual report and an occasional letter from the president. Actually, there are so many stockholders in companies such as General Motors, AT & T, and IBM that there is no indoor place in America large enough for all of them to meet at the same time.

What's My Stock Worth?

Your fortune goes up and down as the price of the stock you bought goes up and down. But what causes this? Here's where opinions diverge, as they say. *Generally* (and that's about the only word that we can use safely here), your stock goes up in value when the company does well (makes lots of money). When a corporation makes a lot of money, management can hardly contain itself and manages to tell lots and lots of people that this has indeed happened. As a result, all of these folks are supposed to rush out and buy the stock (which, of course, pushes its price higher). It's a pure supply and demand game most of the time (that is, with the exception of cheating, shady accounting, great public relations, and mass hysteria).

Other things besides making money can make stock prices rise (and fall too). Sometimes a company can create an impression that it *will* make money (you can use the word *lie* if you like); this can put buyers into a frenzy and push the stock price up too. This of course is highly illegal, but then so is smoking pot in most places. At other times, the stock market gets in a sort of psychological whirl (like the auction where your Aunt Maude's old broken-down butter churn was bid up to $575), and stock prices go sky high for a while. Sometimes the whole stock market (literally thousands of stocks that are traded every day) will fall as a result of bad overall economic news, wars, or sex scandals, and even though the individual company in which you bought stock is doing just dandy, its stock will fall too. It's sort of like rowing down a river; you go faster when the current is swifter. All things considered, however, when your company makes bigger bucks its stock price rises and vice versa.

The Market—What Do They Mean?

We've been talking about your stock, the ten shares you bought in Southwest Turkey Egg Candlers, Incorporated. If Southwest Turkey is a fairly large, high-class company, its stock is traded (bought and sold) generally on one of three exchanges: the New York Stock Exchange—strictly for big outfits, with mega-sales; the American Stock Exchange—for middle-size companies with middle-size sales, just like Goldilocks and the three bears; and the Over the Counter Exchange—for smaller companies with relatively small sales (in relation to GM, not to a lemonade stand). These three exchanges don't handle the stock of all the corporations in America; there are probably half a million much smaller companies whose stock is just not bought and sold in an organized way—rather, in private deals you might say. We're not going to say anything more about these half a million companies because, in my best judgment, you should avoid them like the plague.

Turn on your TV, listen to the noon news on the radio, pick up the morning paper, and you'll see mention of the Dow Jones Average. The Dow is only one of several averages (or "indexes") that measure the overall behavior of stocks on a certain exchange, in this case the New York Stock Exchange (insiders call this "the big board"). The Dow actually measures the average price of thirty selected (hopefully representative) industrial stocks. The Standard and Poor's Index (Poor is not necessarily an evil omen here) measures the price behavior of 500 New York Stock Exchange stocks. The New York Stock Exchange Index and the American Stock Exchange Index are two more indexes that measure the performance of stocks on these two exchanges; and the National Association of Securities Dealers Automated Quotations (NASDAQ) Index tracks what's going on in the over-the-counter market. Thus, it's quite easy to see *how a stock did*, but as we shall see, nearly impossible to tell *how it will do* in the future.

When folks refer to the "stock market," they *can* actually be referring to three different markets. Generally, when the big board flops, all the other exchanges flop too. However, as I noted previously your stock *can* go up when the market is going down, or down when the market is going up. Both these behaviors may be difficult to explain, but the former is much more fun to talk about with your friends.

Do Folks Make Money in the Stock Market, Coach?

They sure do—and millions of dollars too. But that's not the right question. The pertinent question here is "Can *you* make money in the stock market picking individual stocks?" Here the answer is much fuzzier! We can still answer with a tentative "yes," if you meet these conditions:

- You have lots and lots of time to find, research, and pick stocks.
- You have the financial background necessary to evaluate individual stocks (accounting, finance, statistics).
- You have the required information system (personal computer hooked up to data sources) to back up your research.
- You can tolerate the losses that often accompany gains (you know, "what goes up must come down").
- You subscribe to appropriate financial research services (a couple of these are mentioned in Chapter 15).
- You have exceptionally good luck over long periods of time.
- You have access to the kind of talent, information, and manpower that large financial institutions use to play the market.
- You have temporary blind dumb luck for a short period of time and you sell out in time to capitalize on it.
- You discover a "system" to play the market which has eluded experts for two hundred years.

Enough of this silliness! I said it already. Some folks who are professionals do it well and make megabucks. Some folks who are not professionals make bucks too (often for reasons that they cannot explain). But most folks like you are better off never trying to pick individual winners. The simple truth is that the risk is too high! If you just absolutely, positively *must* play in the stock market, we'll show you a much safer way to do it in just a bit, but for now, stay away from picking individual winning stocks—most of us flunk the foregoing test. Besides, you already know that you can reach your wealth goals in a much more sensible (less risky) way.

But I'm Still Not Convinced I Can't Do It by Myself, Coach!

I'm not surprised one bit! This shows high self-confidence on your part and strong intellectual inquisitiveness, too. But let's look at what some of the real experts say. (This wisdom comes from those who *have* made a pot on Wall Street, the folks we ought to listen to!)

Back in 1973, Burton Malkiel (respected high-level financial player and later Dean of the School of Organization and Management at Yale) wrote a terrific book called *A Random Walk Down Wall Street*. He said that the great majority of financial *professionals* would be better served throwing darts at the stock market pages to pick stocks than trying to apply their own strategy. Malkiel suggested that for most of us the market is unbeatable, and that our ability to predict which way it will go or which stocks will do better than the market is about the same as our ability to predict the weather a few days hence.

That's heady stuff (and not everyone believes Malkiel), but there's more. In his classic investment book *The Money Game* (1969), Adam Smith, pseudonym for another Wall Street heavy hitter, said, "If you don't know who you are, the stock market is an expensive place to find out." Still another clever observer of the market was one Fred Schwed, who wrote *Where Are the Customers' Yachts?* way back in 1940. Fred was fond of telling the story of a visitor to New York's financial center. His guide pointed out "There are the bankers' yachts, and there are the brokers' yachts." The visitor then asked, "But where are the customers' yachts?"

Should you pick stocks yourself? Not unless you first pass the test back on page 205. Even then, the risk that they can and will go down is real. But if you are worth $2 million, what do you care—you just pick another one. If, however, you have $20,000 accumulated toward your wealth goal and you buy 100 shares of Amalgamated Fleecing at, say, $200 a share, on a tip that wool clothing cures the common cold, and tomorrow wool is found to cause curvature of the left index finger or something even more bizarre, and Amalgamated Fleecing falls to $2 a share, you are now four years behind in your wealth creation strategy. Of course, it could have worked out the other way too. Amalgamated Fleecing could have doubled in price. I hope it did!

The Coach Has a Few War Stories for You

Education is a wonderful thing. Keeps me employed as a professor for one thing. But my stock market education has been unusual. Back in the sixties, a friend and I started a company that wound up in a few years making a fair bit of money (lower six figures, as they say). A lawyer acquaintance of ours suggested that we take it public—you know, make a million or even two. Well, we did just that! We "converted" our little company to a public company by several trips to New York, lots of money paid to a Big Eight accounting firm to make our homemade books look "uptown," even more money paid to lawyers and the investment house that "got us public." I watched (with fascination) while our still basically little company became public and began to trade, and I could not believe it when the stock went up ten times it original value in less than two years! Here I was, back in Chapel Hill, half of this piddling, mundane, back-country, nothing-much-to-do operation, and the stock was going to the moon. Scared me so much that the first chance I had to get out, I cashed in. I didn't make millions, mind you—the laws on new ventures were just too restrictive back then to make that much. But I cashed in nonetheless for what I thought was good money—at least more than I had ever seen in my life to that point! I never looked back, and I hope those who bought are now worth $7 billion each, but I never forgot either what an unmitigated column of smoke the whole deal was. More to the point: I didn't want any part of a market that could do *to* others what it did *for* me. I don't think you do either.

But time goes on and you forget many of the things you vowed you'd never do. I kept observing what my top few really great entrepreneurial MBAs did when they graduated. I watched their little companies grow, go public, make money, and prosper. So I adopted for a period of time this simple stock market strategy. I'd buy stock (not a bundle, but $10,000 or so) in some of the startups my best MBAs created, and watch. That has turned out to be a very successful strategy. I get brains, guts, discipline, and a few dreams *plus* an MBA. But I was in a very unusual situation in which I could examine carefully over two years the makeup of the person heading the company and guess how that person would operate in business. And it *still* took luck! You probably are not in a similar rare situation, you probably don't know who runs the company, you probably are number 117,865 on the list of folks who get up-to-date information about the company, and—please remind yourself of this often—with relatives like your cousin Sherwood working there, it just isn't the same!

Third war story: Here I sit in front of my typewriter looking back at one of the biggest runups in the stock market since we've been keeping records. The Dow started rising in August 1982 and has risen more than 230 percent as of the third quarter of 1987. During this five-year period, the market value of all stocks has risen just shy of $2 trillion! And you know what? I haven't owned one dollar of stocks during that entire five years. The biggest bull market in modern times and I have been left out! How do I feel? I feel *great*! My wealth plan is on target without the Dow; I have slept exceedingly well throughout this entire five years; I have made a few bucks in investments that make sense for me; I haven't risked a single dollar in the market (maybe some in other places, but not in the stock market); I am happy for my friends who made money and sad for those who lost; but most of all I am doing what we believe makes the best sense for Charlotte and me to do—our own financial schtick if you please! Oh yes, I almost forgot to add that the current bull market *has* been exceeded—that's right, stocks *have* risen even farther than this one. It was between 1921 and 1929 when stock prices rose over 300 percent—you remember, just before the greatest stock market crash in history! Up to 1987, that is!

Final war story: On October 19, 1987, the Dow Jones Average fell 508 points in the biggest crash ever on Wall Street. When the carnage was toted up, investors had lost half a trillion dollars in one day.

Big investors lost; little investors lost; everyone lost! If you had stocks on that day, you shouldn't have. But it is impossible to predict events like that and it will always be so.

No scare tactics. Just these simple facts for you to consider:

- What goes up always comes down.
- Picking individual stocks is a game for full-time professionals, and even they fail often (history verifies this).
- It would have been nice to have made bucks on a stock that rose, but it would be excruciatingly painful if it fell and took

your wealth creation plan down with it (the pleasure you would have felt can't come close to balancing out the pain you would have experienced).

- You can get where you want to be without being an individual stock picker (this whole book is about how).
- If you like stocks, mutual funds are better than individual ones (hang on).
- Cousin Louis' tips are probably worth about what you pay for them.

But 47,000,000 Americans Own Stock, Coach!

True! At least they own stock *or* shares in a mutual fund. So there must be a time when it's right to own an individual stock, you say. Well, you're right; here are a few situations in which you *can* consider individual stocks:

- When someone gives it to you as a gift (if that happens, don't screw up a good deal by quoting from this book; take the stock and sell it if you want to, but take it first!)
- When your company lets you buy stock in it at a fraction of its value (if you *like* the company's prospects, or if you can

buy it and resell, then do it—you may lose, but say the company pays half and you pay half; then the stock value must fall by 50 percent for you to lose)
- When you have an option (a right to buy a stock) at a price substantially below what it is selling for today; you don't have to have a Ph.D. in financial theory to see that buying it today and selling it tomorrow will make you money
- You belong to a "stock club" where everybody puts in $10 a month and buys stock with the money. Be careful to join one where (1) they play poker during most of the meeting and (2) they serve food. That way even if you don't eat much and if you break even on poker, you can hold your annual losses to $120—not too painful. If you know a little about poker and eat a lot, you can come out well ahead, regardless of what the market does. But if you know that much about poker, why are you buying individual stocks?

That reminds me of a story. This one comes from Fred Schwed, a very clever man whom we mentioned earlier. He tells us that playing the market (trying to win by picking individual stocks) is like playing poker. "'Now, boys,' said the hopeful soul, 'if we all play carefully, we can all win a little.'" If that's your strategy in poker, maybe you ought to try eating more at the stock club meeting—that's the *only* way you'll win!

CORPORATE BONDS (WE HEREBY PROMISE TO PAY)

This Sounds Suspiciously like Something We Said Earlier

You get a gold star for memory if you remember that we *did* mention bonds earlier: first U.S. Government bonds in Chapter 9, then tax-free bonds in Chapter 10. All of which means that this is going to be a very short section of the book! These two earlier excursions into the bond business introduced bonds as super-safe U.S. Government-guaranteed investments and as municipal tax-free bonds.

Besides the feds and county and city governments, there must be a hundred thousand or so corporations that issue bonds to borrow money. If you buy stock in a company, you become one of its owners—a tiny one maybe, but an owner nonetheless. When you buy a bond, you become one of a corporation's creditors. You are lending money to the company in exchange for which you will receive interest (that is, if the company makes good on the bond). If you own stock, and the company prospers, you usually get dividends, and the value of the stock rises. If you are a bondholder and the company prospers, you get the same rate of interest they promised you when you bought the bond, and nothing more.

Tell Us about Risk-Return Again, Coach

Corporate bonds are considered riskier than U.S. Government-guaranteed bonds. We generally assume that if the world comes to an end the government will be the last functioning corporation around. Due to the increased risk of corporate bonds, they pay a higher rate of interest than do U.S. government bonds. If, say, a twenty-year government bond is paying 8½ percent today, the interest rate on corporate bonds of similar maturity may range from slightly higher than 8½ percent (very large, very safe, generally very old, most always very financially strong companies) all the way up to 13 percent (interest rate paid on bonds often called "junk" bonds to finance takeovers and do a lot of fairly risky things). You get what you pay for—it's never any more complex than that!

Buyers of bonds have yet another risk to contend with—the market risk. Say you buy a $10,000 bond that pays 10 percent interest. And say that interest rates rise next year, this time to 15 percent. Then your bond is simply not worth as much today, since folks can go out and buy one themselves yielding 15 percent. Thus, if you look at *The Wall Street Journal* for the value of your bond, you should not be surprised to see your $10,000 bond worth now about $6,667. It works out something like this:

$$\frac{X \text{ (the unknown)}}{\$10{,}000} = \frac{10\%}{15\%}$$

$$15\%\, X = 10\% \,(\$10{,}000)$$

$$X = \$6{,}667$$

Now, you are sure to be mad as hell if you read that your bond is worth only $7,000 or so, but wait; the company *did* agree to pay you back your $10,000 if you held the bond till maturity. If that's four years from now, you'll eventually get your $10,000 back, but pray that you don't have to sell the bond in the meantime.

A couple of financial outfits (Moody's and Standard and Poor's) make a living by "rating" bonds. Actually, they give each issue of bonds a grade, which varies from AAA to C. The theory is that if you buy AAA bonds, your risk is less—but you could have figured that out by looking at the rate of interest they pay, couldn't you? Also, the grade doesn't tell you whether the company will ever pay back the bonds, *only* that as far as the rating company can determine, the issuing company is *presently* doing well enough to pay off the bonds. It's sort of like when a prospective employer comes in my office and says, "Professor Levin, tell me what John Jones will do for our company ten years from today." I say he made a B, he looks intelligent, he writes English fairly well, he seems to give reasonable answers to complex questions, and he dresses conservatively. Now if John goes to work for this company and loses a million dollars for them next week, was that my fault?

Is What You See What You Wind Up Getting?

Some bonds are issued with a "call." This means that the issuing company can redeem them (pay them off when it suits their purpose). You can read that as "when interest rates fall and the company can borrow the same money cheaper, they will dump you." If you buy bonds, try to get ones with a call protection; this guarantees the interest yield for a certain period of time.

Other bonds are called "variable-rate bonds." Here, the company promises to pay you an interest rate that varies based on something, often the U.S. Government treasury-bill rate, sometimes the rate of inflation. If you wander into this maze, be careful to check how often they change the rate, and whether they put a cap or ceiling on it (regardless of interest rates in the marketplace).

Believe It or Not, There Are Bonds that Pay No Interest

A few years ago, something called a "zero-coupon bond" was born (about twelve miles west of Storm Warning, Iowa). These are bonds that pay no interest at all, but that sell at an enormous discount from their face value. It works like this: You by a $1,000 zero-coupon bond, but you pay only say $300. You hold it for nine years, at which time the company gives you $1,000. If you go back to Chapter 4 and put on your quant-jock beanie, you'll see that this is an interest rate of about 12 percent. Not bad, you say, but why all this skulduggery? Why not just issue a regular bond that pays interest every year or even twice a year? That's a good question. There are two possible answers. The first is that, financially, the whole thing comes out the same anyhow, so it doesn't really make any difference. The second answer is more interesting. If all of the cars in America were black, how long would it take some enterprising marketing person to decide that painting some cars red might increase sales (or at least might increase the market share of Dynamic Automotive, Inc.)?

I Thought Convertibles Were Cars

Some corporate bonds are called convertible—no, the top doesn't come off, but during the life of the bond they can be exchanged for the common stock of the company that issued them. Two comments here: First, I have already advised you to stay clear of trying to create wealth by picking stocks yourself. Second, the mathematics, finance, and risk associated with convertible bonds is heady stuff. Put this all together and it comes out "no"! Think of it this way: If you believe that mountain climbing is absolutely not for you, and someone comes along and offers you a chance to climb Mount Everest while wearing a bathing suit, just send them packing, okay?

Wrap

Buying bonds from corporations locks you in, so to speak, for a number of years. Most large corporations don't go broke, but some get in serious trouble—remember International Harvester? It was once the fifth largest company in America. Remember too our arithmetic exercise on page 212. It is often painful to get your money out before you planned (of course, this is true of government-guaranteed bonds too). Then consider the difference between corporate bonds (not guaranteed) and government-guaranteed notes and bonds. If the difference is substantial in favor of the corporate bond, examine *very carefully* the risk you are about to take. And don't tell me that there is no extra risk; we have long since classified that response as wishful thinking. If the interest rate is much higher, they know something you don't. Or maybe you *can* outfox the entire financial community after all! All things considered, buying individual corporate bonds is generally not going to be your cup of tea.

PREFERRED STOCK

The first thing you need to do is to disregard the adjective "preferred." This is like referring to lima beans as "sweet." Preferred stock is a combination of the characteristics of common stocks and bonds. The rate of interest the company promises to pay you on your preferred stock is usually fixed, and in the event the company goes belly-up, you get in line, ahead of those who hold common stock, to be paid out of what's left (if there's *anything* left). Preferred stock generally doesn't have a fixed date on which it comes due, although some issues do have a "call" provision (like the ones we talked about earlier) that allows the company to buy you out (generally when it suits *their* purposes). Some preferred stock issues *are* also convertible into the common stock of the company.

Preferred stocks are generally less risky than common stocks. That's because, as we said, when things deteriorate in the company, you get paid off before the common stock holders. But often that's about as much of an advantage as being number 102 in line in the Holland Tunnel instead of being number 127 if the tunnel roof collapses under the river!

Preferred stocks are like the color green. They have neither the piercingly sharp color of blue (one of green's ingredients, you will remember from grammar school) nor the bright cheerful sense of yellow (the other). Unless you buy a convertible preferred, it doesn't have the appreciation potential of a common stock or the lower risk of a bond. It's the worst of two worlds! No one I know really touts preferred stocks as the right kind of investment for those who are trying to accumulate some wealth on a salary. If somebody calls to sell you some of these, let the air out of his tires.

MUTUAL FUNDS (THERE IS SAFETY IN NUMBERS)

Mutual funds are groups of similar investments managed by professionals (people who wear suits and look as if they know what they are doing, who sell stock in their fund to folks like you and me). All things considered, these people (and their funds) do better than you can hope to do (unless you are highly exceptional) trying to pick stocks by yourself while riding home in the car pool with the radio going. For that reason, you need to pay close attention here. If you want to become a player in the "market" (sounds big-time, doesn't it?), then mutual funds are the only way for you and me to go.

There are about as many mutual funds as Jethro's army, but fortunately they are divided into groups not quite as numerous as the major and minor prophets. Let's take a quick look at *some* of the kinds of funds (groups of investments) that enterprising fund managers put together:

- *Growth Funds:* funds that invest in what they call "high-quality common stocks"—no guarantee promised, of course
- *Income Funds:* funds that invest in corporate bonds and sometimes common stocks that pay high dividends (public utility companies and stuff like that)
- *Balanced Funds:* a split in holdings between common stocks and fixed-income securities such as bonds and preferred stocks; you get some chance from the common stocks that your part of the fund will go up and some chance from the bonds that your part will earn income, but you also get some chance that stocks and income will go down too
- *High-Growth Funds:* funds that invest their money aggressively, meaning that they take chances with yours; they are out for big gains in common stocks, so they take big risks to get them—of course, since they invest in many stocks, they do not put all of your eggs (or theirs) in one basket
- *Money Market Funds:* funds that invest your money in a group of generally short-term fixed-income investments including bank certificates of deposit and short-term notes issued by corporations
- *Tax-Exempt Funds:* funds that split up their money in tax-free bonds and stuff issued by municipal governments, as we reviewed in Chapter 9
- *Tax-Exempt Money Market Funds:* a variation of the money market fund, which puts money into shorter-term tax-free municipal notes, and things like that
- *Start-up Funds:* funds that put money into new ventures—very risky stuff
- *Off-Shore Funds:* funds that split their investments among a group of companies operating out of the United States (variations of this include funds investing only in specific geographic areas and even in a single country)
- *One Industry Funds:* funds that invest in just one industry—chemicals, for instance
- *Energy Funds:* funds that buy stocks in companies involved

with energy (generating it, researching it, distributing it, even trying to find it)

- *Real Estate Funds:* funds that invest their money in real estate, of course
- *Option Funds:* funds that play the most dangerous game in finance with the hope that they will generate the highest return doing it
- *Precious Metal Funds:* a family of funds that invest in precious metals and companies that mine precious metals

Only imagination (and space in the financial press) limit the number of mutual funds available today. Actually, there are about 1,300 individual funds that report their value in *The Wall Street Journal* daily. Whatever your investment proclivities, you can probably find a fund that does what you want with your money.

Why Are You High on Funds, Coach?

Careful now, I've never said I'm high on mutual funds, just that most of them can choose stocks better than you can individually. I'll go you one better. If you want to invest in the stock market as a *part* of your wealth-creation strategy, funds are the *only* way to do it. I still haven't pushed you into the market this way, nor will I. It's just *not* the best long-term wealth-creation strategy for *you*. But if you can stand the risk of the stock market for part of your holdings, then funds are the best way to play. Why?

- They reduce the risk of single stock investments because they invest in *many* different securities (stocks, bonds, notes); although it's possible that all of the 100 stocks a fund owns will fall on the same day, it's not too probable—or as probable that all three of yours will.
- They offer you professional, full-time management staff who are trained to invest intelligently and *most* of whom have reasonable records of doing it successfully.

- Funds let you get your money out on any day—you'll remember we called that "liquidity" in an earlier chapter. Of course, if the fund's securities have dropped, you may take a bath when you get out, but at least you can get out your share of whatever's in there (less the money it costs the fund to operate *and make a profit;* yes, Virginia, they don't do it for fun or beer chips).
- They have access to about 987 times as much information about what is going on in the financial market as you do—maybe even 1,346 times as much!
- They are mostly honest people who try to make money for you.
- Funds handle so much money that they tend to do it fairly efficiently—that is, their cost of investment, reporting, and handling complaints from irate fund stockholders is fairly low.

What's It Cost to Play the Fund Game?

Some funds charge a commission for buying the fund (right up front). Someone has to earn a commission on everything that is sold—cars, washers, whatever! These funds are called "load" funds. The commission is somewhere between about 4 and 8.5 percent, depending on about a thousand different things. Load funds generally sell through stockbrokers; some have their own sales force. Both of these types employ people who have to eat and make rent and car payments, hence the load. Other funds, called "no load," don't have this front-end charge; they generally sell directly to you—through the phone, ads, stuff like that. This doesn't mean you get anything free; it means that whatever cost there is of selling to you is hidden somewhere in the reports and brochures they send you. As you would logically expect, new-product development folks being as clever as they are, we now have "low load" funds too—sort of like Plymouth, Dodge, and Chrysler—lots of standard engine, transmission, and electrical parts, but a different body trim. Low-load funds generally stick it to you for something less than 3.5 percent when you buy in.

Funny thing, load funds have had a bigger market share than

no load funds. Funny, too, is that a *Wall Street Journal* sponsored study of 542 stock funds found that no-load funds did slightly better than load funds in 1986. Not entirely new stuff though. Way back twenty-five years ago, a Wharton School research study concluded that "higher sales charges were not indicative of superior performance." This all sounds as if we've uncovered a free lunch, pay less and get more. But have we? To be certain, we'd have to examine how efficiently the fund operates—after all, what it spends on its staff, cars, phones, travel, entertainment, and offices comes out of what its securities are worth. The ratio we ought to look at is called its "expense ratio"—the sum of what it spends to run itself divided by its total assets. A 1985 study found this ratio ranging between 0.28 and 5.3 percent for all stock funds; the average was about 1.3 pecent. What does all this mean? Just that you can call it commission, you can call it sales fee, you can call it maintenance fee, or you can call it chicken. Someone (generally you) pays it! Ah ha! Still no free lunch.

Do Funds Get a Report Card?

You bet they do! For $20 (which will probably go up just as everything else), you can get from the American Association of Individual Investors, 612 North Michigan Avenue, Chicago, IL 60611, the "Individual Investor's Guide to No-Load Mutual Funds," well worth the price if you believe funds are your cup of tea. It's a bit heady in places (talks about stuff like betas—a measure of risk) but it does give you a ten-year report card. From the same address for about a tenth of what that will cost you, try a list of about 250 no-load funds with details on each of their investment objectives. Finally, some well-known business publications including *Barrons, Business Week,* and *Forbes* publish report cards from time to time on how funds perform (how good they are at picking winners). Of course, yesterday's winner can be today's nag, as they say at the track.

Of course, for no charge at all, you can get a quarter of a ton of fancy brochures extolling the virtues of various funds. All you have to do is let someone hear you have money to invest.

How Do I Make a Choice, Coach?

- First, be sure in your own mind what your investment objectives are; if you want to be a part of the energy scene, don't invest in a Far East manufacturing fund.
- Second, examine your own risk preferences very carefully. If you are in for high growth (which I cannot believe after 219 pages), but an aggressive growth fund, but know exactly where you are playing, please, on the risk-return curve—in case you have forgotten, you are way up in the upper right-hand corner.
- Third, don't buy and sell one fund for another. This is expensive (we told you how much on page 218). It's okay to invest in several different funds with different objectives, but stick with what you have. All of the funds are swimming in the same river, and when the current is strong and dead against them, even the best swimmers lose ground for a while.
- Fourth, be sure to get the report card on the fund (or funds) you are thinking about buying just like we showed you on page 219.
- Fifth, read all the fine print and the small print, and the small fine print, and the bold print too before you send a check. See how you get your money out and how long it usually takes. See what charges there may be to get money out. See if they have a toll-free phone number so you can get answers (and service) cheaply. See whether the fund levies a 12b-1 fee on you. This fee allows them to take as much as 2 percent of the fund's assets each year from the money they invest to pay for costs associated with their growth—a very strange deal. Don't let them do it to you.

When you've done all this, go back and ask yourself three questions: *Question 1:* How happy would I be if my money doubled next year? *Question 2:* How sad would I be if I lost half of my money next year? *Question 3:* Is the answer to question 1 (measured in happiness units) bigger than the answer to question

2 (measured in despondency units)? If the answer to question 3 is yes, call the person who represents the fund in your broker's office (or the toll-free number) and, as Vaughn says, pull the trigger.

HOW DID FUNDS DO ON BLACK MONDAY, COACH?

Lousy is the short answer. When the market crashed on October 19, 1987, most mutual funds crashed with it. Remember my story about rowing down the river. When the current is swift, it carries all boats downstream with it! Even the smartest fund managers took a bath on October 19th.

Life Insurance: As an Investment, You Generally Have to Die to Win

Down went the owners—greedy men whom hope of gain allured:
Oh, dry the starting tear, for they were heavily insured.
W. S. GILBERT

FUNDAMENTALS OF A VERY BIG BUSINESS

There is about $6 trillion (that's twelve zeros, count them: $6,000,000,000,000) worth of life insurance in force in this country today. And the industry sells somewhere near $900 million worth (only eight zeros: $900,000,000) more every year. If you really like to cipher things up, that's about $60,000 worth (that's four zeros: $60,000) for every family in the country. Right away, we see that this is a huge industry, and we see that a lot of folks like the product! But many people like lima beans, which I have always regarded as an invention of the devil, so popularity and value are not synonymous in all minds.

Life insurance is a legal contract. It promises to pay you (the insured) an amount of money on the occurrence of a specific event, *usually* your death but sometimes another event such as your reaching a certain age or your having paid premiums of a certain total amount or for a fixed number of years. *And* life insurance is divided into two major categories; the distinction between these is vital, so look sharp!

1. *Term insurance*: This is *pure* insurance—you have to die to collect any money. If anything else happens (an unusually long life, ingrown toenails, skin warts, or two divorces), you don't collect a cent. Term insurance accounts for about 12 percent of the total policies in force in America.
2. *Permanent insurance*: There are about a thousand different kinds of permanent life insurance policies that promise to do good things for you *even if you live*. The companies that sell these kinds can agree to:
   - Create a savings account for you out of your premium payments
   - Tax-defer some or all of these savings

- Spend some of your premiums on stocks, bonds, mutual funds, and stuff like that and manage these for you
- Give you cash (as an annuity) when you retire
- Lend you back some of the money you have paid them in premiums (let you borrow against your money)
- Pay you a certain amount if you die (but generally if you bump yourself off, or have it done for you, you collect zilch)
- Give you free insurance when you've paid premiums for a certain number of years

Permanent insurance, in its many forms, accounts for about 88 percent of insurance in force today.

WHY AM I TALKING ABOUT LIFE INSURANCE IN A BOOK ON WEALTH CREATION?

I have badgered you for a dozen chapters now on ways to save money, invest money, actually everything but steal money so that you can achieve wealth-creation goals that make sense to you. I haven't promised you that you can get rich in the real estate business on $10 of capital. And I think I have been honest in steering you *away* from mad stock market speculation. What I *have* tried to do is to show that a consistent investment strategy over time in fairly low-risk investments (where the numbers work out in your favor) is exactly what makes sense for most readers of this book.

Term insurance is insurance against death—you die, they pay. No savings, no investment, no value unless you die. This is a simple, cheap, and very effective way to provide money to someone who would need it if you died. Just what the doc ordered for most folks! Permanent insurance, on the other hand, complicates the issue by adding a "savings" feature to term insurance. It is a combination of insurance and investment. Part of the money you pay in premiums buys you insurance against dying (just like term insurance); but the other part of your premium goes to create a savings account for you, a stock account, a bond account, a mutual fund account, and yes, Virginia, even a real estate investment account.

Thus, the savings part of permanent insurance (the part of your premium that gets invested) is a wealth-creation strategy that competes with all the others we've covered in this book. Unfortunately, however, it's generally a poor one for most of us. But because the life insurance industry will pitch you hard to buy permanent life insurance (in *some* form) as a way to create wealth, we need to examine it here on its merits.

THEN MAYBE I DON'T NEED ANY LIFE INSURANCE AT ALL, COACH

Whoa! Don't get confused between *whether* you need life insurance and *what* kind to buy. They are two *very* separate decisions. So far, we've been talking about what kind it pays to buy, but since you brought it up, let's switch gears for a page or so and examine whether you need any at all. After all, every dollar you spend on life insurance is a dollar that could be invested in some other way to achieve your wealth goal.

Life insurance ensures against the *risk* that's created if you die—*not* risk to you (you'll be dead and have no risk) but the risk to those who stay behind. If you are single with no living relatives who depend on you, then your death, albeit a sad event, would not really inconvenience ("put at risk" we could say) anyone you leave behind; therefore, you do not need *any* life insurance (I'm assuming you leave enough money in your checking account for a modest funeral, although most cities will bury you free even if you don't). At the extreme other end, if you are married with nine kids under thirteen years old, have a handicapped spouse, support both sets of parents, and are putting a niece through college, you would be sorely missed if you left this earth! Actually, that's not exactly correct. What we *should* say is that your *earning power* would be sorely missed. Whether *you* would be is beyond my knowledge.

So what do we see? Just that you buy life insurance only if your death would create a risk, a hardship, a real set of problems. If it wouldn't, you don't buy. They weep and grieve when you

die, but you don't buy! These rules are very simple. Projecting from this premise, here are some of the situations where insuring someone (like yourself) makes very good sense:

- You are the major income provider for the family.
- Your spouse is unable to work or unable to provide needed income.
- The family owes lots of money on home, cars, and furniture, most of all of which would be repossessed if the income provider died.
- You have accumulated lots and lots of money and the estate taxes your family would have to pay if you died are enormous.
- You and your family have no economic needs, but you'd like to leave a lot of money to some charity, a college, or a person (this assumes they can wait for the money).

And using the same logic, here are the rules when you *don't* insure someone:

- Never insure a child (if he/she died, there would be plenty of grief, but other than funeral expenses, absolutely no risk to those who remain).
- Never *bet* that you will die unless you fully expect to die (avoid expensive flight insurance at airports).
- Don't sign up for credit life insurance on small loans unless you are very old and/or terminally ill; those are the only ways you win here and if you think about it carefully, this is *not* in conflict with what I just said above.
- Never buy a life insurance premium to accomplish something that savings can do (saving for a child's education, for example).

"INSURANCE POOR"—WHAT DOES IT MEAN?

Beginning when I was a year old, my mother (now 87 and as feisty as they come) insured me for $500. I remember what folks call the "depression years" when the insurance man came around every week (Friday as I recall) to collect the 45 cents. And I remember what 45 cents could have bought them, too—ten loaves of bread, forty pounds of potatoes, a shirt, one tenth of a bike. We were strapped financially, not dirt poor, but often out of good food, always out of new clothes, and no bike until I was ten. Time warp now: When I was in my thirties, my mom gave me this same $500 policy for me to cash in. Charlotte and I had a house, two cars, a few bucks in the bank, and most of the bills were paid. The $500 meant little or nothing financially to me at that time—but the memories of what it could have bought thirty years earlier and what tradeoffs Mom made every week to pay the premium, and what pleasures and needs of hers were foregone to insure a risk that just didn't exist made me especially sensitive about being insurance poor.

The evidence suggests that too many of us *are* insurance

poor. We insure risks that don't exist, we bet that we can beat the life insurance mortality tables, we use life insurance for purposes it was never designed for. The result is that our ability to create wealth is impaired because too much of our otherwise investable resources go to pay premiums. Insure the risks that you believe would occur, yes, but *only* those! Right after you read this chapter, your life insurance agent calls on you and tries to sell you a $500,000 policy as "a cheap way to create wealth." After all, he says, the premium at your age is only $560 a year! And look at what wealth you can create on this. You already have all your real risks covered, but you sign up anyway. You have made two mistakes: (1) you have to *die to create the wealth* he refers to, which, if you reflect on it, is quite stupid, and (2) you deny yourself and your family the value, joy, and pleasure of what the $560 a year could bring now! Go back and read this section again!

SPOTTY HISTORY

Okay, you've thought it over and decided that the maximum life insurance you need to cover all of your present risk is $250,000. But you're still not persuaded that term insurance is the best bet for you. After all, you reason, why shouldn't I insure risk *and* invest to create wealth, all in the same permanent insurance policy? For starters, insurance companies rarely tell you what portion of your premium goes to pay for the term insurance part of your policy, and what portion goes into savings. And they generally don't tell you what interest rate they pay on the savings part either. Now why wouldn't someone wanting to sell you something composed of two parts want to tell you what each of the parts costs? Got it? Listen up. A study of the life insurance industry done by the Federal Trade Commission back in 1979 (it was called "Life Insurance Cost Disclosure") concluded that the industry paid an average of only 1.3 percent on insurance savings. Worse, *the industry then got Congress to pass a law that prohibits these kinds of studies.*

The "Life Insurance Cost Disclosure" study we referred to found these rates of return on various investments at that time:

Permanent life insurance held 5 years:	– 9% to – 19%
Permanent life insurance held 10 years:	– 4% to + 2%
Permanent life insurance held 20 years:	2% to 4.5%
Bank pass book savings accounts:	5.25%
U.S. Treasury bonds:	6.99% to 7.67%
High-grade corporate bonds:	8.02%

Draw your own conclusions!

There's more: sometimes, if you cancel your permanent policy (maybe your risk has diminished or your earnings situation has improved, lots of good reasons), you can pay substantial penalties (in other words, give up part of your savings). If you do this in the first couple of years after you buy the policy, there may be little or no savings there at all! Read the fine print. Read it twice. Ask questions if you don't understand something. But don't buy or sign anything until you understand everything. And get competitive quotes!

Most folks are very smart. And for the reasons we've enumerated, lots and lots of savvy insurance buyers have switched to rock-bottom priced term insurance. After all, if you die they pay, no matter what company has the policy! Since the industry couldn't make nearly as much money selling term insurance (you've already figured out that if they paid you only 1.3 percent, they probably could double your money even if their investment adviser was blind drunk under water), insurance companies began to introduce permanent policies with more attractive investment return rates. After all, if McDonalds can't hire all the kids it needs to run at minimum wage, it raises the wage until it can. Supply and demand govern everything! Today, if you shop around, you can buy a permanent policy with a much more competitive savings rate. Hooray for informed consumers acting together!

WHAT'S IT COST, COACH?

That's a hard question to answer with just one number, but it needs an answer! Term insurance rates go up as you get older.

After all, term is *pure* life insurance, and the mortality tables show that your chances of dying increase with your age. But enough equivocating, you asked for an answer and an answer you'll get. Say you're about age 35, and you are interested in buying life insurance. Here are comparable prices:

$100,000 of Life Insurance at Age 35	
Term	$200/year
Permanent	$1200 to $1400/year

I'll say it again, term insurance rates go up as you get older. The same 35-year-old man or woman who pays $200 a year for $100,000 of term insurance (that he or she can renew) will pay $500 to $600 for the same coverage when he or she is fifty and $1,200 to $1,400 when he or she is sixty. In the meantime, of course, the insured has invested the difference between what he or she pays for term and what he or she would have to pay for some form of permanent insurance containing a savings feature.

DO US A COUPLE OF NUMBERS, COACH?

Say you *are* the 35 year old we've been using as an example, and that you *are* considering purchasing $100,000 of life insurance. To compare term with permanent insurance, you need the premiums for both cases. We've shown these in the following table for a period of twenty-five years:

	Premium		Difference saved
Age	Term	Permanent	(permanent − term)
35	200	1,300	1,100
40	300	1,300	1,000
45	300	1,300	900
50	500	1,300	800
55	800	1,300	500
60	1,200	1,300	100

Now, if we take what you save from buying term insurance each year, and if we assume that you can invest that at 8 percent fairly risk-free (you assume whatever you want when you do this) and if you remember most of what we said in Chapter 4, you'll see that by the time you're sixty, your savings should amount to something near $75,600. And you've had the benefit of the *same* insurance coverage you would have with permanent insurance. How do we compare the two alternatives? Just see what the *company* offers as the value of your savings in their *permanent* policy after twenty-five years. If it's more than $75,600 guaranteed, and if the other terms in the policy are to your liking, consider it seriously. If it's less, buy term and save the difference yourself. Be sure to check whether the savings in their permanent policy accumulate tax-deferred! Many policies do exactly that, and if that's the case, you must account for it in your comparisons. What fancy footwork did we do to get the number $75,600? None really; we set up a simple little table for twenty-five years, subtracted the term premium from the permanent premium each year, and compounded the difference saved for the appropriate number of years (twenty-five years all the way down to one year) and added up the values. The whole exercise took less than five minutes. If you have a personal computer, you can probably write a program and do it in fifteen minutes.

FAIR IS FAIR, DICK

One of my very good friends, Arthur, who is a very successful life insurance general agent (that's someone who has lots and lots of salespersons working for him) would have me shot if I stopped here! And he's right. There are some recent developments in permanent life insurance forms that suggest that you should never make a decision on life insurance lightly—rather, that you should take the time to work out the numbers carefully. After all, if you are young and considering a policy in the neighborhood of half a million dollars, the amount of money involved over your lifetime is huge! Hint: It's worth fifteen minutes with Chapter 4!

"Universal life insurance" is a ubiquitous term these days. If you sign up for one of these policies, you generally get insurance coverage plus a rate of return on the savings part, with the interest tax-deferred till you withdraw it. That's not a bad deal. But it's not all that unique either—you can do the same thing yourself! Just buy term insurance, and invest the difference in a tax-sheltered investment such as those we covered in Chapters 8, 10, and 11. Is that better, you ask? We can't say without crunching the numbers. Ask your agent what her company guarantees as its interest rate, figure out the tax savings, compound the difference between that and term, and tote it up—simple as that. The biggest number wins! I'll give you help on a special version of this in a minute.

ODDS AND ENDS, THINGS TO WATCH

Many insurance policies that provide tax-deferred savings don't guarantee interest rates. Of course, in their defense, trying to forecast interest rates has sent many a financial wizard to the funny farm. Interest rates *do* change, and when you're doing your "figure work," be safe rather than sorry—estimate them on the low side, especially if they appear in the insurance company ad in big print. Make sure whether the interest rate that is quoted is net of sales commissions and administrative charges, too. And if you do go the "permanent" route, make sure you can borrow against the value of your savings in the policy without tax consequences—and without waiting an eternity either. When you need money, you need money.

Finally, there's a new twist in life insurance forms, the single premium policy, which offers tax-free yields and insurance coverage combined—a special form of universal insurance. This policy has only one premium—that's right, you pay the *whole* premium for the entire life of the policy in one lump sum when you buy it. You can borrow against the policy with no tax consequences. In many cases, as long as you are borrowing against interest the policy has earned, and not against your original premium payment, your loan is interest-free. The savings part of this policy can be tied to a mutual fund, in which case your return depends on how well the mutual fund's investment adviser does. This is very heady stuff for most of us, and if you can afford to put down $25,000 cash as a single premium, maybe you should buy a cheap term policy, and turn back to Chapters 8 through 11 and figure out what to do with your $25,000. Permanent insurance is probably *not* the answer.

DISCIPLINE I AIN'T GOT

All during this dissertation on how to compare the cost and benefits of term insurance with permanent insurance, we've kept you busy investing the difference between the two premiums. This, of course, assumes that you haven't spent it. I know a lot of folks who, at thirty-five years old, would buy a cheap term policy for $200 a year and instead of investing the $1,100 difference (look back at page 232 if I am confusing you) would just throw it away! If you are one of these, a "closet financial wastrel," then you could have saved yourself a lot of time, grief, and eye strain by bailing out on the first page of this chapter. If you just aren't up to the consistency and discipline it takes to invest that difference, then there *is* no problem and there are no alternatives to evaluate. You just buy the cheap term policy and throw away the difference. If anybody criticizes you, just call him an over-disciplined, phlegmatic, formalistic, systematic, unimaginative, financial dullard. That's worse than a wastrel!

QUICK AND DIRTY REVIEW

For most of us, insurance is for protecting others, *not* for saving or creating wealth for ourselves while we're alive. And most of us don't really have the money to make huge investments in single-premium policies. So, the general rule is buy term and invest whatever you can of the difference. Do the numbers, yes. Don't ever buy more than you need and unless you know something that only you and your doctors know, and that no insurance company doctor can find, don't bet that you can beat the odds. Oh yes, and be sure to read all the fine print, too. Twice.

14

Getting the Family in the Act

Taxed on the coffin, taxed on the crib,
On the old man's shroud, on the young babe's bib,
to fatten the bigot and pamper the knave
We are taxed from the cradle
plumb into the grave.
REPRESENTATIVE THOMAS R. HUDD OF WISCONSIN, 1888

SIMPLICITY LOST—THE TAXMAN COMETH (AGAIN)

If the I.R.S. in its wisdom taxed everyone at the same rate (say, for instance, if every man, woman, and child in the country paid 20% of their income in federal income tax with absolutely no exceptions), then this chapter would be just about over. All we would note was that your employer multiplied what you earned by 20 percent and sent a check for that amount to the feds—then stand by for Chapter 15. A five-line chapter would look pretty silly; but, true to form, the federal government in its roughly two hundred years of existence has never done anything easy or logical, and what could be five lines is eighteen pages after all. It's a good thing, I guess. Imagine 235,687 tax advisers out of business, straining already pressed welfare programs. And without our complex tax code, what would newspapers and financial journals use to fill the pages and pages of tax advice and tax analysis and tax updates they publish today? No, folks in Washington will never simplify the tax code, but their constant tinkering with it amounts to guaranteed full employment for tax lawyers and accountants. Maybe some of it will trickle down. Meanwhile . . .

THE LAW AND SOME NUMBER DRILLS

At this writing, the tax law looks like this. (Don't blame me when all these numbers are out of date within two years—write your Congressman! But remember the principles; they'll keep a while longer.) Just find your place in the filing categories that follow and pay what it says there:

Folks Filing Single Returns

Taxable Income Between	Is Taxed at This Rate (%)
$0—$17,850	15
$17,850—$43,150	28
$43,150—$100,480	33
Over $100,480	28

Drill problem: Suppose you are an individual filing a single return, and your taxable income is $54,000; what federal tax do you pay? Simple:

On the first $17,850, you pay 15% which is	$ 2,678
On the income between $17,850 and $43,150 (which is $43,150 − 17,850 = $25,300), you pay 28%, which is	7,084
And on the income over $43,150, which is $54,000 − 43,150 = $10,850, you pay 33%, which is	3,581
For a total of	$13,343

which comes out as an effective (a term meaning "true") tax rate of

$$\frac{\$13,343}{\$54,000} \quad \text{or} \quad 24.7\%$$

Married Folks Filing Jointly

Taxable Income Between	Is Taxed at This Rate (%)
$0—$29,750	15
$29,750—$71,900	28
$71,900—$149,250	33

Drill problem: Suppose you are a couple filing a joint federal tax return, and your taxable income is $62,000; what federal tax do you pay? Simple again:

On the first $29,750 you pay 15% which is	$ 4,463
On the income between $29,750 and $62,000 (which is $62,000 − 29,750 = $32,250) you pay 28% which is	9,030
For a total of	$13,493

which comes out as an effective (a term meaning "true") tax rate of

$$\frac{\$13{,}493}{\$62{,}000} \quad \text{or} \quad 21.8\%$$

Married Persons Filing a Separate Return

Taxable Income Between	Is Taxed at This Rate (%)
$0—$14,875	15
$14,875—$35,950	28
$35,950—$113,300	33

Drill problem: Suppose you and your spouse file separately—perhaps for one of the reasons we'll examine in just a little bit. If your taxable income is $41,000, what federal tax do you pay? Easy if you do these steps:

On the first $14,870, you pay 15%, which is	$2,231
On the income between $14,870 and $35,950 (which is $35,950 − 14,870 = $21,080), you pay 28% which is	5,902
On the income between $35,950 and $41,000 (which is $41,000 − 35,950 = $5,050), you pay 33%, which is	1,667
For a total of	$9,800

which if you divide by your total taxable income turns out to represent an effective tax rate of

$$\frac{\$\ 9{,}800}{\$41{,}000} \quad \text{or} \quad 23.9\%$$

An Unmarried Head of a Household

Taxable Income Between	Is Taxed at This Rate (%)
$0—$23,900	15
$23,900—$61,650	28
$61,650—$123,790	33

Last drill problem: Suppose you are an unmarried head of a household filing your federal return and your taxable income is $32,000; what is your tax bite? These two steps will get an answer:

On the first $23,900, you pay 15%, which is	$3,585
On the income between $23,900 and $32,000 (which is $32,000 − 23,900 = $8,100), you pay 28% which is	2,268
For a total of	$5,853

which comes out to an effective tax rate of

$$\frac{\$\ 5{,}853}{\$32{,}000} \quad \text{or} \quad 18.3\%$$

What do these number drills tell us about federal tax? First, although there are only three tax rates (15, 28, and 33 percent), the effective tax rate you pay is determined not only by these rates but also by the category under which you file (single, married, married filing separately, or single head of household). This fact caused our four effective tax rates to come out to be weird numbers like 24.7, 21.8, 23.9, and 18.3 percent. As you have already figured out, this means that your effective tax rates can be anything between 15 and 33 percent. Actually they can be between 0 and 33 percent, but you have to earn $0 income to get the most advantageous rate. Second, because the category under which you file *does* have an effect, it becomes an important tax consideration. We'll say more about this in a while. And third, we've proved our earlier contention that regardless of what the Congress says it intended, it still hasn't come up with something as simple as three rates.

ARE THE NUMBER DRILLS OVER YET, COACH?

Unfortunately, no. Uncle Sam has some very specific words about how he will tax kiddies, too. Here, the effective tax rate depends on four factors: (1) how much the tyke earns, (2) how he or she earns it, (3) how old he or she is, and (4) at what rate the child's parent pays tax. The result of all this mumbo-jumbo is a tax table that looks like this:

The Kind of Income the Kid Has	For Taxable Year in Which Child is	
	Under 14	Over 14
Earnings (salary, income from odd jobs like fixing up your duplex, income from delivering newspaper)	Taxed at child's tax rate	Taxed at child's tax rate
Investment income under $1,000 (interest, dividends, generally money earned on money you gave them)	$500 not taxed; rest taxed at child's tax rate	Taxed at child's tax rate
Investment income over $1,000 (same kind of stuff as above)	Taxed at parent's tax rate	Taxed at child's tax rate

What does all this kiddie mumbo-jumbo mean? It means that very often shifting income from you and your spouse to your kids can result in a lower effective tax rate *for the family*—because, relatively speaking, you're taxed high and they're taxed low. It also means that if you have children, and if you want to involve them for tax purposes (the new national pasttime), you have to do some clever tax planning and, of course, watch their ages. Suppose you and your spouse have a six-year-old child. And suppose you give this child a gift of $12,000 and invest it for her in a very safe 8 percent account. It earns 8% × $12,000, or $960, a year which means that your daughter pays federal tax (here comes a tiny bit of bad news: if the child is five or older, she will have to have a social security number and file a tax return if she has more than $500 of investment income or earns more than $2,540) of:

First $500 of income is free of tax	$0
Next $460 ($960 − $500) is taxed at the child's lowest rate filing individually which is 15% for a tax of	69
For a total tax of	$69
and an effective tax rate of $\frac{\$69}{\$960}$	7.2%

Do we have your attention yet? Did that 7.2 percent figure wake you up? Are you ready to sit up a couple of nights filing tax returns for all your little tykes? (Or, better yet, get your accountant to do it?) Listen up.

Had you and your spouse decided to invest the money yourselves, your tax on that $960 of interest income would have been something between 15 and 33 percent, depending on your taxable income. And the feds don't care who gave the child the money. There's more! These amounts that the child will be able to earn and still pay tax at low rates on will be adjusted for inflation beginning in 1989.

HOW TO BE SMART—AND LEGAL, TOO!

Regardless of the age of your child, it makes good tax sense for him or her to generate the highest possible income (at least the highest he can earn or you can arrange to provide through investments) until the point at which his or her income is taxed at a rate higher than yours! After all, the child has to have a taxable income higher than $29,750 for his tax rate (15 percent) to rise to what yours probably is (28 percent) assuming you file jointly. Check the tax tables on pages 240 and 241 if this confuses you. Of course, if you are a pauper and your child has somehow managed to amass a fortune that generates investment income of a million or so a year, he or she would be smart to arrange for you to get some (you pay taxes on it) because your tax rate starts at 15 percent and the child's is way up there at, say, 33 percent.

If you have children under fourteen (remember, if they earn investment income over $1,000, they pay tax at *your* higher rate), it makes good sense to defer their income until they are fourteen and can pay tax at their own (child's) rate again (15 percent). You can do this by buying a U.S. savings bond that matures after the child is fourteen. If the child is thirteen and a half and has investment income-generating potential over $1,000, you can even buy him or her a Treasury bill that matures after he or she is fourteen, and save tax that way.

CAVEATS

You're sitting there with four children (14, 15, 16, and 17) and you've already figured out that if you give them your entire wealth to invest ($200,000), they can invest it at the same rate you do (say 8 percent) and earn the same $16,000 you have been earning on it, but pay taxes at about half the rate you have been paying (15 percent versus your 28 percent). (And if you do it over three or four years, you can escape the gift tax on the $200,000 too.) Your greedy little mind has already ciphered that this ploy saves almost half of the $16,000 in taxes annually. Great, you are smart, you are practical, and you have understood this chapter well! But, suppose your children take the $200,000 and charter a Boeing 747, and take 375 of their friends to Brisbane, Australia, for a rock concert. Where does that leave you and your wealth? Oh, you say, I know my kids better than that. Great, I say, but if half of the family warfare that occurs on the soaps is true, maybe you should chat with your attorney about a legal agreement that will protect the children from the money, the children from the lawyers, you from the children, the money from the children, and the crowded courts from four more lawsuits!

And finally, there's one more caveat. Splitting income (that's what we've been doing for a few pages now) requires you to maintain some records and file some reports. We've already noted that each child would require a social security card, but that's no big deal. They all would have to file income tax returns, again no big deal for you to do for them since with only investment income, their returns would be quite simple. They would have to keep some minimum financial records (tax returns, bank records, investment records, stuff like that), and none of that is too onerous either to save $8,000 a year in federal tax.

GOODBYE KIDS, HELLO BRISBANE

Call it what you will, but the principle is taking off big piles and putting on little piles. Divide and conquer. A little taxpayer goes a long way. United we stand. All of these slogans make good sense under our tax laws for those of you with children—or those who are contemplating some. Whenever you find a way to pay tax at 15 percent when you've been paying tax at about twice that, pay attention! Besides, the current penalty for failing to include a social security number on your child's tax return is only $5. And, after all, your children and their 375 friends would get a lifetime of memories and social maturation experiences from that rock concert in Brisbane.

HONOR THY FATHER AND MOTHER

Under the current tax law, you can claim an elderly parent as a dependent as long as you provide more than half of his or her support. It doesn't matter whether your parent lives with you; only the amount of support you provide counts. If your parent files a tax return (and remember that many don't because of their very low income), sit down and cipher up what the total tax bite would be under the two alternatives: (1) your parent files a return, and (2) your parent doesn't file and you claim him or her as a dependent. In the latter case, those medical expenses that your parent incurs (but doesn't claim as deductions) can then be claimed by you; even though they may not be substantial themselves, they may raise your *own* medical expenses such that the total is more than 7.5 percent of your adjusted gross income, and therefore permit you to claim a medical deduction that you would have otherwise lost. These are small benefits, but they add up! Remember compound interest!

MORE BREAD—BIGGER BENEFITS

If you have the money, you can give your parent up to $20,000 a year without paying a gift tax (only $10,000 if you file a single return). She can then invest the money, and because of *her* lower tax rate (she probably would pay only 15 percent federal tax) get by with lower taxes than *you* would have paid on the money. If you are supporting her anyhow, this is a smarter way to do it. At the time of your parent's death, you get the money back without estate taxes (unless your parent is worth more than $600,000 when she dies). This can be a major wealth-creation benefit to you. For example, say you give your parent $15,000 a year that she invests, and say that you and your spouse are paying 28 percent tax on your income. Since your parent probably pays only 15 percent tax, she saves you 13 percent tax (28%–15%) on whatever the $15,000 earns. If it earns 8 percent, her investment income is $1,200 the first year, and 13 percent saved on that is $156. Not much you say. Well, not much for *one* year, but give her $15,000 a year for fifteen years, add up all of the taxes you'd save from doing this, and see if you don't come up with a total tax saved of about $2,295 compared to what you could have done by yourself at your tax rate. And we haven't even counted interest on what she saved you; compound the tax saved and 8 percent interest and in fifteen years you are just shy of a total of $4,575 ahead of where you would have been by yourself.

Let's get real fancy for a minute. Suppose your dad (age 66) lives on social security and a modest level of support from you, $3,000 a year. The money you give to your father is after-tax (you already paid the tax on it) and since you provide *less* than half of his support (his social security is about $5,000 a year), you can't claim him as a dependent. With your eight-year-old son to educate, things look tough! Try this. Set up a trust to last ten years, sufficiently large so Dad can receive the $3,000 a year he needs. At say, 8 percent interest, this would take

$$\frac{\$3{,}000}{0.08} \qquad \text{or} \qquad \$37{,}500$$

Let Dad get the interest for ten years (he'll pay *no* federal tax because after sixty-five he's permitted to earn $5,650 of non-social security income without paying tax). At the end of ten years, your son will receive the assets of the trust ($37,500) tax free for his college education. Of course, if there is any fear that dear old Dad will take the $37,500 and charter a Lear jet and take six of his friends to Paris to see the new Lido show, maybe you ought to see your lawyer first!

LOVE WORKS IN BOTH DIRECTIONS, TOO!

Perhaps your parents or your spouse's parents have some money and want to help the two of you without making you an outright gift. This is financial double talk for "I don't want any of your money because it creates dependency, and besides John will get angry that I am taking money from my parents." There are a couple ways that your parents can help themselves while helping you—as we've said once before, doing well while doing good!

First, they could buy a house that you and John want and then rent it to you. Your payment covers all of their expenses (see Chapter 11); they get all of the tax deductions (we covered this in Chapter 11, too). The only kicker is that you and John do not create any equity—just a pile of cancelled rent checks. Of course, you get to live in a home you probably can't afford, with a very small probability of being evicted if you miss a rent payment, too! In this deal, your parents get all the financial benefits.

Second, if you want to create some equity in a home (which means create some wealth) and have the income for half the mortgage payment but don't have the savings you need for the down payment, try this version. The feds will permit what is called a "shared equity contract." It takes a written contract, but lawyers have to eat too. You and John put up, say, half of the down payment and your parents put up the other half. They own half of the house, you and John own half. You and John get to deduct your half of the mortgage interest and property taxes from your taxable income, while your parents get to deduct half of the depreciation, insurance, and repairs since they are investing in the house while you are only living in it. You pay them a fair market rent (no tricks, please) on their interest in the house (if a whole house of this quality would rent for $900 a month, then "half a house" should rent for about $450). If you and your parents decide to sell the house in due course, each of you gets half of the proceeds. The "ownership split" can be just about anything. Much *less* than a 50 percent share for you and John, and you are back "living off your folks' largesse" with its attendant vicissitudes; much *more* than 50 percent for you and John, and you probably can't get up the money for the down payment.

See a lawyer, listen to the lawyer talk, watch the meter run, get everything in writing. If you believe that your parents will evict you on a bitter cold, snowy night, when you are five days late with half the rent, buy a smaller house all by yourself.

SHOULD WE DO IT TOGETHER, JOHN?

Sometimes, just sometimes, married couples can make a few dollars off of the feds to help them along the way to their wealth-creation goals. It takes a keen eye on your tax situation and a bit of arithmetic. Suppose someone stole your $20,000 car and it was not insured, and you didn't get it back. This is called an "unreimbursed theft loss," and to the extent that it exceeds about 10 percent of your adjusted gross income, it is deductible, thus reducing your taxable income. If you and your spouse each have high incomes and file jointly, then 10 percent of your combined adjusted gross income is a bigger number, making it wise for you to look at the benefits of filing individually and letting your spouse do the same. You'll both pay a slightly higher tax rate if you do, *but* maybe, just maybe, the uninsured loss will result in a total tax bill for the two of you that is less than if you filed jointly. This requires some arithmetic, yes, but maybe some bucks saved too!

The same goes for big medical bills suffered by your spouse. Medical expenses are deductible only to the extent that they exceed 7.5 percent of your adjusted gross income. Again, if you and your spouse file jointly, 7.5 percent of a much bigger number *isn't* deductible, so it may pay you to file individually. This means more ciphering, but maybe more bucks put away too.

Here are two other very minor reasons for filing separately, neither of which has anything to do with wealth creation. First, if you and John want to keep your financial doings separate from each other (maybe even confidential), then separate returns (with somewhat higher taxes, though) are the route. And finally, if John has been involved in a lot of suspect financial deals lately (drugs, guns, laundering money, illegal shelters) and you think he is about to be arrested by the feds for income tax evasion, then filing separately may, just may, keep your own wealth from being attached (a condition just before confiscation) by the I.R.S. for

John's dirty deeds. These last two deals may make for a miserable marriage, but then you can't buy money with happiness, can you? Nuff said!

DON'T MISS ANY OF THE FREEBIES, PLEASE!

Being single with a dependent or dependents can be the real pits! But single folks with dependents can often qualify to pay taxes at those attractively reduced rates shown on page 242. There you'll see that unmarried heads of a household get to pay tax at 15 percent on income all the way up to $23,900; what's more, you see too that they can earn all the way up to $61,650 without hitting the 33 percent tax rate. So what's it all about? The I.R.S. considers you an unmarried head of household if you are:

- Single, divorced, or widowed on the last day of the tax year
- Your home is the principal residence of the person(s) you claim are dependent upon you for more than half of the year
- You pay more than 50 percent of the cost of maintaining the household

So get out your rent receipts, your food bills, your calendar, and the tax tables on pages 240 to 242 and see if it pays to investigate a little more. The savings are not trivial and can create a good bit of wealth themselves if you qualify.

MY SON, THE PRESIDENT

The tax laws, as we have noted several times in this chapter, make it attractive to shift income from parents to children. And we've shown you a couple of tricks on how to do that with investment income. But if your child is of an age (probably anything over ten) that he or she can be productively employed in some enterprise you run and actually earn money for the value of his or her labors (without you lying, that is), then the strategy is to shift as much income from you to the child as possible. From the table on page 240, we see that the child is able to pay tax at only

15 percent on income all the way up to $17,850; as long as you can legitimately pay your children for working and deduct their wages as an expense, they will wind up paying taxes of 15 percent on income that you perhaps would have had to pay tax on at twice that rate.

Accomplishing this really tests the imagination; imagination is what makes for a good tax attorney, and for a good parent, too! Back in our treatment of real estate (Chapter 11) we suggested that if you went this route, you should employ your child as much as possible to work on your real estate project—the houses or duplexes you own. This would involve painting, clerical work, yard work, collecting rents, fixing windows, going to the bank with deposits, cleaning inside, and just about anything that needs doing. Pay your child a reasonable wage per hour. A bright thirteen-year-old is surely worth about twice what children earn working in a fast-food emporium, but the brightest seventeen-year-old is never worth $25 an hour in the eyes of the I.R.S. Invent work, invent hours, but don't invent overly high wage rates.

If you don't own rental real estate, the advantages may still be there but it takes more imagination. If you do these kinds of things yourself for money either part-time or full-time, then you have all the ingredients necessary to shift income to your children, and thus create more wealth by paying less total tax:

- Decorate
- Paint
- Direct weddings, bar mitzvahs, confirmations
- Carve
- Clean
- Cook
- Cater
- Tend sick folks
- Knit
- Sew
- Do carpentry
- Do plumbing
- Do electrical work

- Tend livestock
- Landscape
- Pave
- Make furniture
- Build homebuilt airplanes
- Guide tours
- Crochet
- Embroider
- Lay carpet
- Write books, articles, monographs
- Make wine
- Make liquor (if your still is registered)
- Install drywall
- Install tile
- House sit
- 10,876 other full-time and part-time occupations that generate income

In each of these cases, there is probably an opportunity to employ one or more of your kids, pay them wages, and let them file a tax return and pay the feds at 15 percent. Your child can help, fetch, watch, collect money, kibbitz, measure, tear out, nail, check supplies, make phone calls, keep records, look, check, get in the way, or generally make a fool of himself, but that's not the point. What is important is that you shift income from you to him and thus taxes from, say, 28 to 15 percent. Taking off big piles and putting on smaller piles—that's the ticket. Sure you have to keep records, pay social securuity, file reports, and do other stuff that perhaps you'd rather not do, but anything that keeps kids off the street, saves taxes, and creates wealth is worth looking into, isn't it? No blood test is necessary; the child doesn't have to interview; his eyesight need not be checked; his labor union proclivities are irrelevant; and he need not take any tests. All he needs to do is show up and work and give you a legitimate excuse for paying him money—the more, the better is the rule!

DON'T MISS THE BENEFITS OF BEING SELF-EMPLOYED

True, it's nice to be self-employed and have no boss giving you a big ration of grief every day; but then having to suck up to your banker, lawyer, customers, creditors, and accountant as an entrepreneur all sort of make up for that, don't they? Actually, one of the nicest benefits of being self-employed is that you can set up your very own (and quite generous) tax-deferred retirement plan. You'll remember we chatted about that first in Chapter 8. Whereas IRAs are no longer deductible from income in many cases, retirement plans that you set up for yourself if you are self-employed are! We call them Keogh plans in honor of the clever guy who invented them. And what's even better, you can make a tax-deductible contribution to such plans of 20 percent of your net self-employment earnings, all the way up to $30,000 a year! Money put in these plans grows and compounds (Chapter 4) tax-free until it is withdrawn. If you take it out early (before you are 59 1/2), the feds kill you (actually it's only severe penalties, not death). These plans are what they call a good deal in the trade. And thus, being able to set up these plans and create wealth tax-free is enormously attractive. Of course, if you go into the business of removing barnacles from the underside of the Lincoln Tunnel and sell them for 10 cents a pound just so you can set up a Keogh plan, they call this stupid, but then we used this example back in Chapter 5, so we'll move on.

IF THIS IS SO GOOD, MAYBE THERE'S A BETTER ONE

The ultimate tax-deferred retirement plan is called a "defined benefit" plan. It comes under the same part of the tax law as Keoghs, but is infinitely more liberal. It works sort of like this: Say you are forty and start your own business; things go well and in a few years you see that your taxable income is $62,000 a year. Being bright, you also see that you and your spouse are paying the feds $13,493 a year. (If you are skeptical, go back to page 241 and you'll see that this is exactly the income figure we used there in our drill example.) How do you reduce the tax bite?

Since you have no retirement plan (except the mandatory self-employed social security one that may provide you $567.81 a month) you can set up one designed specifically for you and your needs. The feds will allow you to put aside each year (tax-deferred) an amount of money sufficient to provide you an income roughly equal to the one you now earn ($62,000) when you retire. They make you figure this out using expensive actuaries, lawyers, accountants, and all that, but they *let* you do it, and that's what's important. The effective upper limit you can put aside tax-deferred is about $90,000 for you (you *can* put away a maximum of another $30,000 or so for your spouse if he or she works for you).

Suffice it to say here that this is a fairly expensive proposition that takes a lot of legal, accounting, and actuarial work, and is probably more than most of our readers will get involved in. But the point is that if you or your spouse *is* self-employed, and *if* you start making some fairly nice bucks, and *if* you are at least forty, actuarially you are a prime candidate for a defined benefit retirement plan. That's because the feds let you forecast your retirement age as 59 1/2 years, and as we have already said, they let you put as much aside each year (tax-deferred) as is required to provide you then with the income you are earning now. And they let you accumulate all this and the interest tax-free until you take it out years later. And if you really want to get a thrill, go back to Chapter 4 and figure out how much you'd have to invest each year at say 6 percent (you *always* use very low investment returns when you figure out these plans—that makes the amount you can defer come out higher). If that really turns you on, call a lawyer or a CPA who specializes in these plans.

WHAT DID WE SAY?

Current tax laws reward those who create wealth by shifting income from big piles to smaller piles (from parents to kids). There are about a hundred legal ways to do this. Current tax laws also reward those who are smart enough to create wealth by getting parents and children involved in tax considerations. There are about half a dozen good things you can do here. Our tax laws also favor those who create wealth by checking tax tables to see which category they should file under (if they have a choice). There is only one way to do this correctly. Tax laws in this country really do favor self-employed folks who create wealth by finding clever lawyers, accountants, and actuaries, who help them set up retirement plans specifically designed for their own needs. There is only one way to do this right. And, finally, U.S. tax laws and tax folks generally dump on people who try to create wealth by lying, cheating, being "too" clever, and doing dumb things. There are about ten thousand ways to do this, but if they catch you, they'll dump on you regardless of which way you used. A word to the wise! Onward.

15

Looking Back, Looking Around, Looking Ahead

What is life, without a dream?—Edmond Rostand

LOOKING BACK

Some Useful Redundancy—What's It Take Again, Coach?

Brains, guts, discipline, and a few dreams. These were what Sim had, and what I think are the basic requirements for admission to the wealth-creation strategies we've thrown at you—or, if you please, the basic colors from which a few practical rainbows can be constructed. If you have these, you are in! *Brains* are needed to figure out the few financial conundrums necessary to evaluate alternatives (just like the MBAs do in the uptown banks) and to choose intelligently among alternatives when your list gets larger than one. And brains are required too to reject the tooth-fairy, get-rich-quick schemes. *Guts* are needed to be able to pull the trigger, as Vaughn said we must do if we are to get anywhere; to stand your ground when your financial train gets slightly off the track from time to time as it will; and to insist on a fair deal from financial folks, and to say "no" when you think you're being screwed. *Discipline* is that remarkable quality that gives you control over your behavior and that organizes it and focuses a lot of little actions over time toward a big goal somewhere in the future. Discipline is also needed to save, to forego immediate pleasure some days for the sake of your wealth creation plan, and to wait patiently while time—and compound interest—both work for you and your goals. And, finally, maybe the most important of the four requirements—a few *dreams*. Without these, the future always looks smaller instead of larger; the goals you set are far too modest compared with your ability; and you don't get to see the future you are trying to create; thus, its fascination, its value, and even its smell and taste are denied you.

And What Is Wealth Again, Coach?

Wealth is how you feel about yourself and what you are doing, not just how much money you have accumulated. Of course, it's okay to think that you are great *and* accumulate a million bucks, too! Wealth for you should be a goal that you think about very carefully and that you set only after a good bit of real soul-searching (both you and your spouse or significant other get in the act). Wealth is never limited to money! Wealth is what money buys for you that gives you pleasure. Wealth can be counted and looked at (Midas was good at this); wealth can be spent, not accumulated (some psychologists call this self-gratification or inability to defer pleasure), but remember my good flying friend Pebbly who died penniless with a smile on his face as he recalled his last sunrise flight. Wealth can be defined entirely in terms of lifestyle—you remember my friend who wants a small house in the country, a truck that works, enough firewood for heat, and to be allowed to practice her profession without giving or taking any shit. Wealth can be toys—houses, cars, planes, clothes, and baubles, if that's what turns you on. And wealth can be defined in terms of self and self-image—getting your nose fixed, your teeth capped, your wrinkles gathered, and even your head shrunk.

Most of the time (actually just about *all* of the time), we wind up defining wealth (at least partially) in financial terms. It's a fact, however sad, that most of the things we'd like, or like to be, or like to cause, or even like to change cost money. Being a penniless hermit who lives in a cave in the woods on nothing is just not practical anymore! Land costs too much; food and vitamins are exorbitant; caves are dank and need heat pumps; and, besides, most of the good caves have been converted into condos anyway. So even though we may dislike the idea of money as a thing of value or something to be valued, we are usually forced to count, to dream, to measure, and to keep score on how well we are reaching our nonmonetary goals by using *money* as a surrogate. If your cave is unlighted, dirty and cold, and if you can't get ABC's *Nightline*, and if you are living off alfalfa sprouts, lichens, and snails, and if you are dressed in mattress covers, then your quality of life is really in question. So we do keep score in money and we do our calculations in money, and we try to be smart enough to realize the limitations of what we are doing, so that we avoid becoming a captive of the "counting system."

And What Were the Things We Were Supposed to Watch Out for, Coach?

Number one on the list was "Don't screw the family"! Every day in your life is a small miracle—and unlike cars with defective brakes, no day can ever be recalled. Behavior is age-appropriate and saving up behavior is about as valuable as saving up air. Don't inventory dreams that must be played out this year to be meaningful. Do it now as long as you can afford it. Do it later if it makes sense to do it later. If not, do something later that *does* make sense. In sum, don't try to con folks you really love by telling them that we are saving all our money to spend when we are old. When you are old, you need laxatives and back braces, not money!

Next on the list was "Watch out for great deals that don't cost much." We entreated you to discard anything that smacked of "get rich quick," "make a million in real estate with three dollars down," and "how I bought Minneapolis with tax-free exchanges starting in Sheboygan." These are all fakes. Sim would have known it without any formal education. Your six-year-old already knows it; and you have to accept it too. There just isn't any way to create wealth that doesn't involve some sweat. Dick's first rule is "There is no free lunch." Dick's second rule is "Go back and read the first rule."

We first showed you rule three with a graph. If you'd like to see it in words, it might be expressed as "The more return you want to earn, the more risk you must take." It's as true as night follows day or as water runs downhill; but even in our advanced society, lots of folks still believe they can find a way around it. Lincoln was right when he said, "You can fool some of the people some of the time." Had he lived today, he might well have altered it to "You can fool most of the people most of the time—with enough advertising." Smart "fast-buck" deal peddlers would paraphrase Lincoln today with "You can fool some of the people some of the time and generally that's enough." High return always means high risk. High return with no risk means you probably have the numbers backwards. Low return with high risk means you probably have your head on backwards!

One More Time, What Are the Good Investments for Us?

Like a dress that fits well, a wealth-creation strategy for those who earn between $20,000 and $70,000 a year must fit well too! Our best advice for you was in Chapters 8, 9, 10, 11, and a part of Chapter 12. We strongly encouraged you to take advantage of every company-matching investment deal or tax-deferred deal that can be invested in "safe stuff" on the logic that if they kick in too, your wealth grows faster than if you do it all by yourself. We strongly touted U.S. Government bills, notes, and bonds on the grounds that they are the safest investment in the world today, while yielding only a point or so less than those with risks that folks in your situation should avoid. We suggested that you investigate tax-free bonds, but *only* after you have calculated (and understood) what the taxable equivalent return is for these. We said then that if you were so inclined, rental real estate was a rather nifty way to make some money, create some value, and get some of your withholding back in the bargain. And finally (in Chapter 12), we said that if owning "a piece of America" was in your blood, then carefully chosen mutual funds were the absolute only vehicle we would sanction! And that was it! No fancy stuff, no high roller deals, no venture capital funds, and nothing with very much risk. This is not timidity, mind you, but a sensible positive choice given who you are, where you want to go, how much you can really afford to lose, and the strong knowledge that most reasonable wealth goals *can* be reached this way!

And That Means That I Ought to Stay Away From?

Stay away from antiques (unless your great aunt dies and leaves you a million dollars worth of these), antique marbles, African tribal drums, bank stocks, cars (antique, racing, touring), daggers (ancient, ceremonial, Japanese), diamonds, elderly care homes, frozen pork bellies (or just about anything frozen for that matter), great works of art (lesser ones too), hammocks (except one for the summer), insurance (except term), iron mines, jewelry (folks get annoyed if you sell this so you wind up wearing and looking at all your wealth), kitchen equipment, land (except the kind under inexpensive houses or duplexes), metal (gold, silver, platinum), money (confederate, foreign, more than you need for monthly transactions), navel oranges (or any other farms, groves, or vineyards), opium (hell-of-a-return but awful risk, too), options, professional office buildings, ponies (and any other livestock except maybe one for your kids), quick-food outlets, rest homes, stocks (individual hot picks, that is), show-biz deals, turkey farms, undervalued standing timber, venture-capital deals (some of these guys are real bandidos), water (lakes, streams, developments on both), xylophones (or any old musical instruments except one for your kid to practice on), orange juice futures, and zirconium (or any precious metal—remember the Hunt brothers).

And How Were We Supposed to Figure Out the Good Deals, Coach?

Dick's fourth rule: "If the numbers don't work out, you are probably screwing up." Without numbers that make sense (to you), you are betting on luck; or worse, on weather; or even worse, on your cousin George to come through for you. In my family, our cousins (some with unusual names like Zalotta) are all wonderful folks, and we love and enjoy them, but not for investment advice. No, we crunch the numbers just as we taught you in Chapter 4; we play quant jock; we see if things work out on paper—with *no* wishful thinking. And if they don't, we immediately become suspicious and start asking nasty questions.

Dick's fifth rule: "If you don't work out the numbers first, you are definitely screwing up"!

LOOKING AROUND

I Looked in the Mirror and Here's What I Saw

Most of our wealth-creation strategies bet on you! True, we do suggest that you get some help from an accountant, lawyer, or maybe even a stockbroker, but you're the driver, the planner, the director, and the one most responsible for the way things turn out. We've already assumed that you qualify on Sim's criteria: brains, guts, discipline, and a few dreams. But there's more! To make all of this work, you need personal honesty, too. When all is said and done, you are still your best investment adviser—who knows better than you what your risk preferences are? Who knows more than you about which things turn you on and which ones provide little value? And who is there for each investment decision, each transaction, each evaluation, and yes—for all the number crunching, too! You, that's who. And thus we make the point again—personal honesty (trusting yourself, never cheating yourself, and above all, never lying to yourself) is vital to drive the investment strategies we've laid out for you. Without it, your decisions can turn out to be inconsistent, illogical, and disappointing. When you've "got it," implementing your own wealth-creation strategy works better!

And What Else Have You Assumed About Me, Coach?

So you're honest with yourself. Great, but not nearly enough! You've got to apply that honesty in practical situations to win consistently. So I've written down in the book of assumptions that you:

- Know or can figure out your priorities for you and your family (things you want, things you want to do, things you want to be)

- Can rank these priorities (lots of hard choices—tradeoffs—here)
- Can relate these priorities to time (what now, what later)
- Will be brutally honest when you figure out how much you can afford to invest (go back and read Chapter 3 again)
- Can avoid the temptation of "get-rich-quick" deals (hardest to do when your best friend just made $5,000 in one)
- Took the time to master the number work in Chapter 4
- Can defer *some* current pleasure without severe mental consequences (without being able to do this, you generally never accumulate much beyond next month's rent)
- Have correctly "classified" yourself (that you are *not* a wild entrepreneur, a backer of long shots, or a closet Russian railroad bond trader, but a salaried sensible person with, you know, brains, guts . . .)
- Believe enough in yourself and your abilities to make these kinds of investment decisions so that you do it instead of letting others do it or wishing they would
- Can sustain yourself from time to time by looking fifteen to twenty years ahead (some folks would call this the ability to "discount dreams")
- Can pull the trigger when the time comes (Vaughn would approve).

It's a list, but not too painful.

LOOKING AHEAD

What's the First Thing I Do When I Finish the Book, Coach?

Be cool, that's what! Sure, I hope you're fired up about wealth creation and I hope you can pull the trigger, but the watchword here is caution (care—prudence—deliberateness). Don't just rush out and sell the family farm or hock the car. Get a cold beer, sit down, read the book again (at least the parts you find useful); think things over, drink another beer, get out a pencil and paper, make a few notes on the plan, begin making lists of things, drink another beer.

Deliberateness—that's the key word! About ten years ago, my good friend Dan (a flight instructor) was helping me prepare for my multiengine pilot license. Now planes with two engines *can* fly on only one, but only above a certain speed, which is known as "minimum single engine control velocity." It's a fact. Lose an engine *above* that speed and you can usually fly merrily on. Lose one below that speed, and your twin wants to turn into a rock. Meaning—you will fall out of the sky if you do not do the right things in the right order on time. Specifically, you must identify which engine quit—not as easy to do as you might think either. If you get it wrong, and pull the wrong levers, you are now flying a "no-engine" plane. To get (and renew) your multiengine license, you have to fly the plane very very very near that critical speed on *one* engine. It is perfectly safe to do, *if* you do it exactly correctly with great deliberateness. As I go through this potentially treacherous maneuver, I always remember Dan's sage advice: "Don't snatch and grab the levers, Dick, get straight in your mind what you are going to do and in what order first." Happily I have followed Dan's advice for ten years now without the twin ever turning into a rock.

So we say to you, don't snatch and grab the levers—have another beer and get your whole situation thought through first. It's like flying the twin: do the right things in the right order and you can fly home safely. Otherwise you go home "vertically" (financial equivalent: lose your shirt!).

Where's the Checklist, Coach?

Right here—and it's not all that long either. Start by rereading Chapter 3, then:

1. Set some wealth creation goals for you and your family that you believe make sense.
2. Make a list of what you own and what you owe—a personal balance sheet if you please.
3. Separate out these assets you are "living in" that you can't

invest—you remember: car, camper, clothes, etc.; what's left after that is your current investment potential.

4. Now make a list of all your income (everyone in the family gets in the act here).
5. Go back through the simple budgeting process we introduced in Chapter 3.
6. Reread the list of 111 ways to save money on pages 48–52 (several beers help here).
7. Cipher up what you can afford to invest every month after you've provided for your family's needs.
8. Make a list of the investments we've covered in Chapters 8 through 12 that are appropriate for you (probably the hardest step of all!).
9. Find out what rates of return they are yielding (for real estate this, of course, will involve doing a fair bit of financial homework).
10. Use the methods in Chapter 4 to test whether the strategies you have picked out achieve the wealth goals you set in step 1 above. If they do, proceed to implement your plan; if they don't, go back and adjust your wealth goals or your rate of savings till they do. (A fatal mistake here is to adjust the investment risk to reach the wealth goals—an absolutely fatal mistake!)

Of course, like everything else in life, it's harder to do in person than in a list in a book. But what was that old aphorism, "where there's a will, there's a way." My dear friend, Rose, is the living embodiment of that advice. To her, *nothing* is impossible, every problem has a solution, ingenuity will conquer all physical barriers, and faith is the glue that holds it all together. Now Rose doesn't accomplish everything she sets out to do (a few even defy the laws of physics); but her deficiencies are those of time, energy, and age—never vision, planning, and hope. My marvelous Aunt Frances (now age 91 and full of spunk), on the other hand, is a genetic naysayer. She knows fifty ways for things to go wrong, forty-three possible events that may keep her from attending some function, and thirteen very good reasons why it will probably rain next August 23. Now, I've shown you mathematically that wealth creation can work for you. To make your own wealth creation strategy work, you need to be more like Rose than Frances. (Of course it helps enormously if you can live to age 91, too!)

Don't Leave Me Hanging Out Here Please, Coach

Way, way, way back in the first chapter, I remarked that there were about 250 books offering investment advice—now that I'm on the last chapter, soon to be 251. All of these were written by very nice folks too, but it's a fact that most don't focus on you—the defined market segment of this book. However, I've gone through much of what's been written on the subject and pulled out a few sources and names that I believe are worth your time. These folks on my list all have something useful to say—I certainly don't agree with all of it, but I never thought the Dow would fall 508 points either!

- *Value Line Investment Survey*: fifty-one years old, with over 100,000 subscribers, this high-end investment advice service reviews 1,700 stocks weekly and says which it thinks are the best. An expensive but good service with a reasonable track record of picking long-term winners.
- The *Wall Street Journal*: daily (except Saturday and Sunday) newspaper of the financial world, yet extremely readable, informative, and entertaining even for financial neophytes; in business for almost a hundred years; excellent way to keep up with what your investments are doing (but don't be swayed by any of the high-return, low-risk ads it runs)
- *Money Magazine*: very clearly written assessments of things financial, pitched more to us less technical folks than other financial publications (lots of articles you'd like and learn from)
- *Business Week* magazine: broad weekly review of the financial (and managerial) scene; data on performance of investments; good for getting a general picture of what's going on financially in the world today

- *Money Angles* by Andrew Tobias: a fine short book with both fundamentals of investing as well as the more esoteric stuff for higher rollers
- *The Power of Money Dynamics* by Venita Van Caspel: a delightful book (a bit dated but now being updated) covering everything from the cut of a diamond to gas-drilling partnerships; great writing style, abundant honesty, lots of good advice.
- *Buy Low, Sell High, Collect Early & Pay Late* by what's-his-name, Dick Levin: another cheeky little book that explains everything you need to know about accounting and finance in 200 pages—cartoons, too, written for folks who hate accounting and finance.

Curtain Going Down

Before I quit and put my typewriter in storage for another year, I want to do five things: make a statement, repeat an aphorism, tell a joke, pay my respects to Sim, and say something personal to you. So here goes.

First, the statement: Of all the things I do professionally, none gives me as much pleasure as sharing ideas with others. Some of my ideas are weird (I was a strange kid); a few of my ideas are new (I had great teachers); most of what I write is about my personal experiences (I have made and lost just about enough money to have the humility to write a book like this); but everything I write is meant to explain, to uncover, to make the difficult simpler, to encourage you to try something new, and to cushion the fall when you take one. I am very lucky to be able to do this and get paid too!

One of the great American writers was Elbert Hubbard. If I told you about Elbert once already, it's okay to do it again. He wrote lots of things, but one will always stick in my mind: "Parties who want milk should not seat themselves in the middle of a field in hopes that the cow will back up to them." Elbert understood human nature. He also understood the difference between dreaming and doing. You need both!

Then there was this old Belle Barth joke. Belle was a great

comedian who worked Miami Beach and always left them rolling in the aisles. Seems there was this destitute 83-year-old couple. He blamed her for all their troubles and insisted she go to work to support them. She asked what he thought she was qualified to do, and after some thought he suggested she try being a prostitute. Reluctantly, she put on her best dress, powdered and painted up the best she could, and went forth on this entrepreneurial venture. Four days later she returned, obviously the worse for the experience. "Did you make any money?" he asked. "Yes," she said. "How much?" he inquired. "Thirteen dollars and ten cents," said she. "My, that's an odd sum of money," he said. "Who gave you the ten cents?" "Oh," she replied, "*everybody* gave me ten cents." So it adds up, you see, just as we said it would in Chapter 4!

Sim had this gold tooth in the front of his ample smile. He also owned an old truck, but I told you that. When I was thirteen, he and I traveled the backroads near where I grew up selling bushel baskets of peaches mostly to poor tenant farmers. Most of our customers were women. Sim drove and I managed the enterprise. He would flash that tooth and that smile and two bushels would go off the back of the truck and four bucks would

hit the cigar box. Then we'd do it again, all day in the heat, all summer. Until I was twenty-one, I believed it was my financial and marketing abilities that made the enterprise the success it was. In fact, it was Sim all the way. He drove, he smiled, he cajoled, he flashed that gold tooth, and he dealt! I was so much excess baggage! God bless you, Sim.

And now I'm done! The rest is up to you, as they say. We've covered a lot of ground, introduced a lot of ideas, ciphered up a lot of numbers, pointed out some things that make sense for you, steered you around some things that definitely don't, and tried real hard to make you see that you can do it if you want to. About the only things left to say are:

1. Thanks!
2. "Parties who want milk . . . "—you know the rest.

P.S. Good luck!

Coda: Ratty Looking Bunch But They Work Cheap

AUTHOR:

DICK LEVIN earns his salary as a teacher of MBA students and executives at the University of North Carolina at Chapel Hill. He builds psychic wealth, in case you missed the 217 references to it in this book, by fishing—last summer for lake trout and northern pike 300 miles from the Arctic Circle. But pompano and blues in the surf off North Carolina make him feel just as rich.

He made his all-time best investment ($5) in a marriage license.

CONTRIBUTING EDITOR:

GINGER TRAVIS is a Carolina MBA, a writer, an editor, and a hippie at heart. She takes some of the advice in this book seriously but not much else. She loves traditional Appalachian string band music and her home in North Carolina.

CARTOONIST:

LAMBERT DER wields his pen and his wit in Greenville, South Carolina, as editorial cartoonist at *The Greenville News*. His cartoons have also appeared in *Time*, *Newsweek*, *The New*

York Times, and *The Washington Post*. A native of Durham, North Carolina, he cartooned *Buy Low, Sell High, Collect Early & Pay Late: The Manager's Guide to Financial Survival*. And Dick and Ginger and some other folks know this book wouldn't have had the same pizzazz without him. Thanks, Lambert!

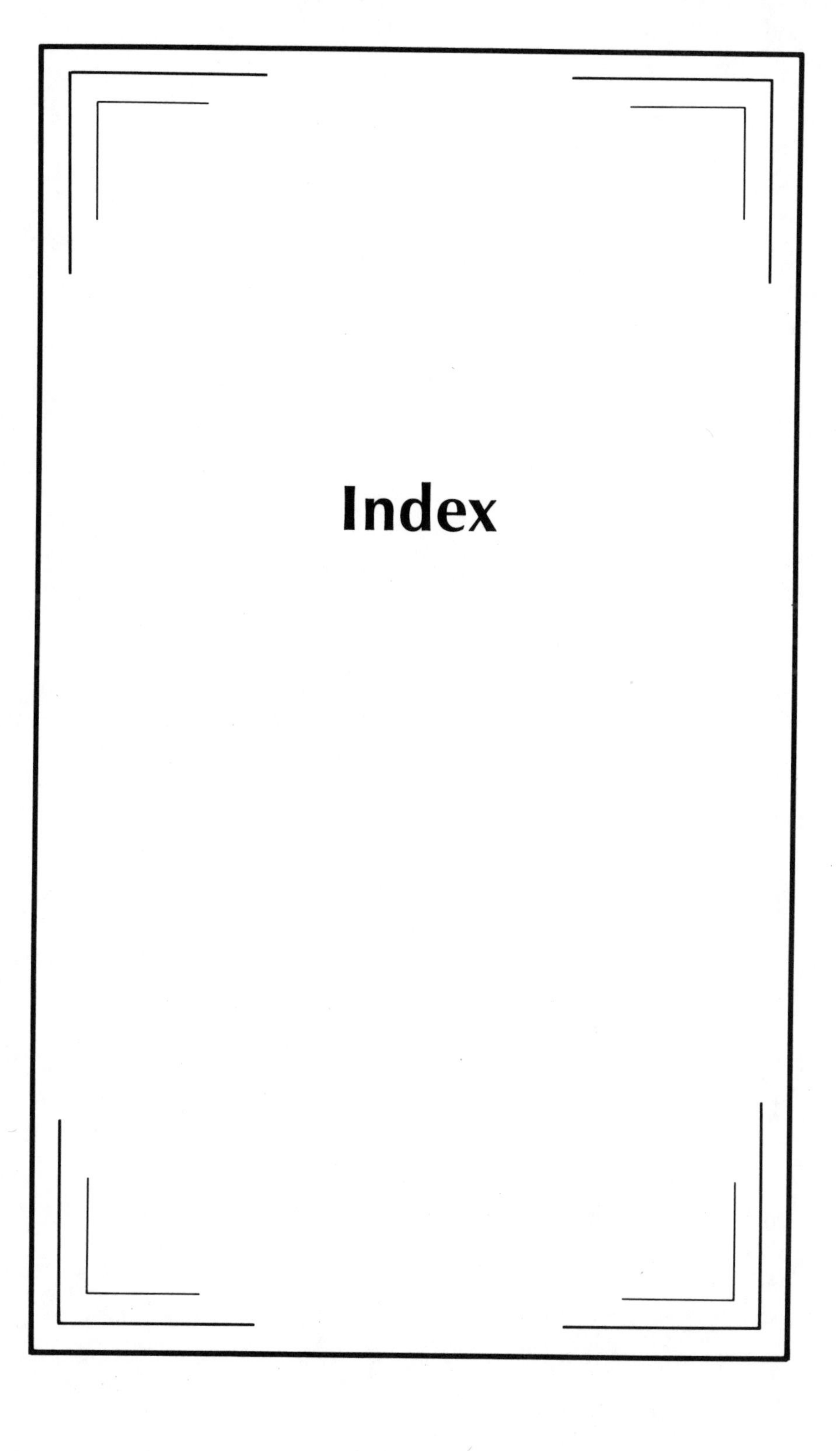

Index

D

E

F

G

H

I

J

K

L

M

N

O

P

Q

R

S

T

U

V

W

Y

Z